I Remember Nonna

by Eleanore Berra Marfisi

Eleanore Berra Marfisi

Ricordate sempre la vita e l'amore della

nonna e tua vita diventera piu bella.

Always remember the life and love of nonna

and your life will become more beautiful.

G. Bradley Publishing, Inc. • St. Louis, Missouri 63131

Eleanore Berra Marfisi strongly believes that the Italian culture and heritage are to be preserved, since what is not preserved is lost forever. The author has been a long-time resident of the City of Saint Louis. She is a retired high school principal who has taught elementary, high school, and college classes. She holds a Bachelor of Arts degree in English and graduate degrees in Art and Secondary Education Administration. She is a member of Pi Lambda Theta Scholastic Honor Society. Her retirement has been spent writing, as well as studying music and art. She is a guest lecturer on topics such as the preservation of the Italian culture. Other titles she has authored include *Italian Roots, American Flowers; Dolci: Italian Sweets; Art-O-Graphs; Jewish Art in Christian Symbols;* and *Sicily: Crossroads of Culture.* Her very popular book, *The Hill: Its History, Its Recipes* was released in 2003.

Front End Sheet: Sister M. Stephanie, A.S.C.J., and the Young Ladies' Study Club do serious research.
Back End Sheet: Bridal shower of Jane Bottini in 1947.

www.gbradleypublishing.com

Table of Contents

Publication Staff

Author: . . . . .Eleanore Berra Marfisi
Copy Editors: . . . . .Blake Baraks
. . . . .Gloria Baraks
. . . . .Faye Venegoni
Proofreader: . . . . .Patricia Merlo
Book Design: . . . . .Diane Kramer
Photo Design: . . . . .Michael Bruner
Cover Design: . . . . .Michael Bruner
Project Coordinator: . . . . .Brad Baraks
Publisher: . . . . .G. Bradley Publishing, Inc.

ISBN 0-943963-99-0
Printed in the U.S.A.

Introduction

It is my sincere desire to honor and to preserve the charming simplicity and deep faith of the Italian-immigrant nonnas. Even several generations away from their homeland, the descendants of those who braved the Atlantic continue to use folk stories, rites of passage, holiday customs, and especially their tantalizing *dolci* dessert recipes to express and celebrate their distinctiveness as Italian-Americans. Their folk tales, home remedies, superstitions, and proverbs are captured in this publication. These stories are told and retold by their children and their children's children. It is always well to remember that we, in fact, through preservation strengthen the future of all children regardless of their ethnic heritage. Note – These wonderful nonnas came from various regions in Italy, thereby accounting for the different quoted dialects.

Reader's Note – All material taken from personal interviews start and end with a ◆. Because of the universality of much of the material, the author has chosen not to personalize the interviews with individual names. Secondly, photos have been selected at random and placed throughout the book as a representation of early life on the Hill in St. Louis for the typical Italian-American woman.

Every House on Every Street

Every house on every street
In every Italian neighborhood
There was a Nonna
Whose kitchen felt the warmth
Of an old stove oven.
Where gnarled fingers
Kneaded flour and yeast and water
Into wondrous loaves of bread
Fashioned into varied shapes. . .
Round, knotted, large and small,
But for special feasts she created
Shepherds' crooks and decorative crosses.
And in every house on every street
A Nonna sliced
The warm bread into huge slabs
Sprinkled them with olive oil,
Salt and a healthy shake of pepper.
And in every house on every street
A Nonna would encourage
Everyone, anyone
To savor and enjoy her bread
While she retold
Tales of every house on every street
In her old world across the ocean.

– Eleanore Berra Marfisi

Nonna and Her Stories

Rosie Ottolini gracefully waits for her photograph to be taken.

very nonna carries her life in the lines of her face. On her features are chiseled the fine lines of every thought, every joy, every sorrow, and every emotion. The early Italian nonna who came to this country did not know what the new world had in store for her.

Rather than feeling lost, she took pride in her new homeland. Perhaps her strength came from the preservation of her past. She never gave up the values she brought with her. Her wisdom will always be the text of the lives of the early Italian-immigrant women.

These women were the glue that held families together. While their men went out and worked with their hands and their backs, it was the women who kept the fires of their lives glowing. More often in the shadows, they were, nonetheless, always the strength that held family values and traditions intact. No one knew this better than their men who often said, *Sembra io che sono il padrone di casa, ma mia moglie é la cuore.* (I may seem to be the head of the house, but my wife is the heart.)

In every household was a wise and wonderful nonna (grandmother), mamma (mother), or a zia (aunt). They are to be credited for preserving the fascinating folklore which is, in essence, the poetry of their lives. This folklore is inherent in the Italian nature. It is tightly woven into the tapestry of the lives of the women, both friends and relatives in close-knit, Italian-American neighborhoods, making it impossible to extricate one from another. Oliver Wendell Holmes once said: "We are all tattooed in our cradles with the beliefs of our people, the record may seem superficial but it is indelible."

Giuseppina LaFerla proudly displays the apples picked from her tree.

Nowhere were fables more revered than by the early Italian-immigrant nonnas who passed on this legacy to their children and children's children.

Folk tales spun by nonna were more than mere entertainment—they were great vehicles of truth that became mighty educational engines transporting their children out of the realm of reality. Imaginations were ushered into wonderlands. Then, quietly and ever so gently brought back to their own little world with beautiful lessons learned. One of the best-loved memories of growing up were the times spent listening wide-eyed to the women spinning tales of magic and fantasy learned from their mothers.

Just a reminder:
All material taken from personal interviews starts and ends with a ◆. Photos have been selected at random for their image appeal and do not connect with the text. Unless noted, all photo names are identified from left to right.

Mary Ronzio kneels alongside daughter Mary Lou who enjoys her Easter baskets.

Maria Griffero pauses after picking her garden herbs. Circa 1930.

Josephine Giustiniano, Grazia Monaco, and Carmela Caroselo don their lovely Easter outfits. Circa 1940s.

The Abandoned Baby

Angelina Torretta, clad in her starched and neatly ironed gingham dress, with cotton stockings rolled to her knees, was one of the Hill's best storytellers. Arranging the folds of her apron neatly about her, she sat on the curbstone under the lamplight and gathered the children on the block around her. What anticipation! Soon a wonderful fable would unfold.

A favorite was about a baby abandoned in the woods.

The LaFerla sisters: Angelina, Giuseppina, Rosa, Marianna, and Concetta enjoy a happy reunion.

◆ One day a crotchety old woman named Maria Cativa (Mean Mary) came upon an abandoned baby. In a rare moment of weakness she took the baby home and named him Antonino. Maria Cativa never went to town and rarely went to church. No one spoke to her because she was so unkind.

In 1896, Rosa Carolli and daughter Maria pose for a postcard photo to send back to family in Italy.

When Antonino was five years old, she took him to town. Maria Cativa needed help to carry the groceries.

She said to Antonino, "While I go to the fish market, you carry the bag with the bread and wine. Wait for me in that church."

Antonino was a very good boy so he hurried off. Never having been in a church Antonino was in awe of the beautiful colors made by sunlight dancing through the stained glass windows.

Walking up the wide, marbled aisle, he looked up and saw a man nailed to a huge cross. Excited, he began asking the figure many questions: "Who are you?" "Who put you up there?" "Why did they do this?"

Quietly a voice said, "I am Jesus." Antonino, feeling so sorry for Jesus asked, "Are you hungry?" Without waiting for an answer, he quickly stood on a nearby bench and gave Jesus his bread and wine. Jesus responded, "Antonino, you have been so kind, is there anything you wish for?"

"Oh, yes," said Antonino. "Please help Maria Cativa to be nice so that the townspeople will like her."

Angelina Coco and Zia Josepina Coronella greet each other with a warm embrace.

At that moment Maria Cativa walked into the church and heard everything that was said. She immediately fell to her knees and promised to be kind to everyone. ◆

Angelina would then turn her gaze on each one of us children and in a hushed voice whispered, "You should all try to be like Antonino. Talk to Jesus and ask Him to help others. Don't be selfish and only think of yourselves. Then Jesus will bless you too.

We never tired of hearing Angelina telling us the story of *Antonino, Pan e Vino.*

Little Carlo

Maria Griffero was a consummate storyteller. She loved to spin her magical stories whenever or wherever she had a young audience. Maria would preface each tale with "They are all true!" (*'e vero!*) We children always begged, "Maria, tell us about Carlin." Nonna Maria, looking intently at each eager face, would say, "Remember, they are all true." Then, we were swept up into her world and the adventure began.

Pierina Vismara Savio (standing) poses with her mother and two sisters in 1948.

◆ *Una volta* (once upon a time), there was a little old man named Carlin (Little Carlo) who lived in the small town of Rubone, Italy. Carlin was a very religious man who always stopped in the church to say a prayer. The people in Rubone said it was good that he did because he had such a bad temper.

Marlene Fagala and her very own "first" car, circa 1940s.

One Good Friday, Carlin entered the church. He walked devoutly up the aisle to kiss the crucifix that had been set up in front of the altar. But when Carlin bent down to kiss the feet of Jesus, his long gray beard got tangled in the crown of thorns. He struggled to get free. Unsuccessful, he became very angry. He screamed and threatened the Lord. Somehow, he finally broke free.

Later that evening he returned for services. The large crucifix had been replaced by a miniature one.

Approaching the crucifix, Carlin shouted, "Aha, because I got mad at you God, you sent your baby Son in your place! ◆

Amid our laughter, Maria smiled, knowing she had once again brought joy to her audience.

The Wolf and the Squirrel

As a little girl growing up in Alia, Palermo, Carmen Floretta loved to visit her grandmother. Nonna Carmela suffered from arthritis, but her pain never stopped her from sitting in her favorite chair, rocking and reciting her stories. Carmen especially enjoyed *Lupo e lo Scoiattolo* (The Wolf and the Squirrel.)

◆ There once was a little squirrel, Giuseppe Scoiattolo, who loved nothing more than to perch on the highest limb of a tree. All the other squirrels thought he was lazy and some even thought he was not too bright. No one wanted to play with him. But little Giuseppe did not care. At least, he seemed not to care.

Gloria Denando is ready for kindergarten.

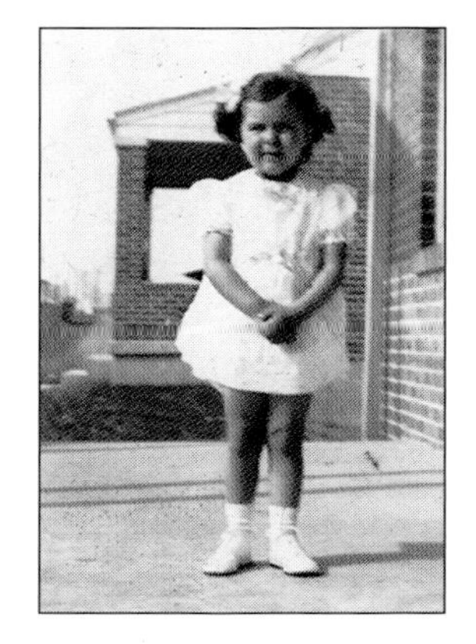

One day as he was jumping from limb to limb he fell out of the tree.

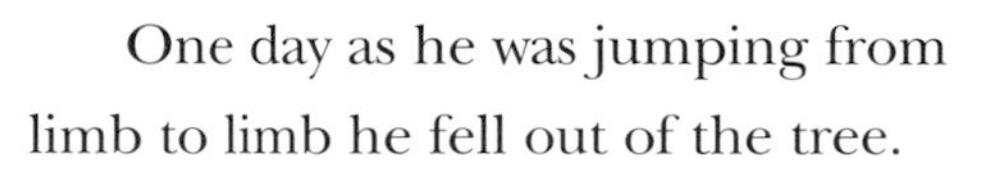

Mamma mia! He fell right on top of a very mean and sly wolf that had been sleeping under the tree. The angry wolf grabbed the little squirrel and was ready to eat him. Frightened, Giuseppe begged and begged for mercy.

The angry wolf said, "If you will tell me where all your squirrel friends are, I will let you go."

The mean wolf thought, "If he tells me where they are, I'll not only have him for supper, but I'll have all the others, too!"

Pleading with the wolf, the little squirrel said, "Please, let me climb up the tree where my little head can think better. Then, I'll be able to tell you where they are."

The wolf consented and Giuseppe

Lillian Foglia, a lovely little flower girl in 1940.

Emilia Fontana Garavaglia obviously enjoys being a grandmother.

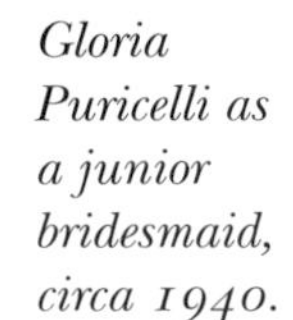

Gloria Puricelli as a junior bridesmaid, circa 1940.

scampered high up to the very top of the tree. When he was safe he called down. "Senor Wolf, you are not so smart as you think. I may not be as sly as you but I am safe up here." Giuseppe, the little squirrel, laughed as he playfully tossed acorns down on the wolf's head.

From that day on all the other squirrels admired and played with little Giuseppe Scoiattolo. ◆

Then Nonna Carmela would gently say to little Carmen, "Cara mia, we must never judge anyone and never think we are better or more intelligent. *Siamo tutti figli d'Dio!* (In the eyes of God we are all His children!)"

Young ladies enjoy a dance without their men who were serving their country in 1942.

What could be more enjoyable than a trip on the Admiral *with friends? From left: Eleanor Pisani, Marie Brusatti, Mary Neri, and Theresa Vago.*

In the Land of the Monachichi

The early peasants from Calabria, Italy told wonderful fables. They believed in tiny creatures much like the leprechauns. These little people were called *monachichi*. They were extremely mischievous and tormented and harassed small children. Whenever anything went wrong in the town, the *monachichi* were often blamed. Because they were so sly, they were never seen.

◆ My grandmother, Mariangela, who was a

Calabrese, would tell me about them. She was a very religious woman, but folk religion had become intermixed with her Christianity. Before going to bed she would say her rosary. Then she would come sit at my bedside, and tell ghost stories and tales about the little people, the *monachichi* - stories that she actually believed of dead people's spirits visiting a sleeper. As a child I found these stories frightening but I knew my grandmother loved me and would keep me safe. The following is one of the tales.

Mary Fontana and her little brother David enjoy a stroll.

One day in a little town in Calabria, Giovanni, a mischievous boy, ran away from home because he had forgotten to tend the fire and his mother scolded him. Tired of running, he sat under a tree when he suddenly came upon one of the *monachichi* who was called Pepe. Now Pepe possessed very special powers. Upon spying Giovanni he planned to lure the boy into the land of the *monachichi.*

"Giovanni," he called, "Come walk with me. I have something to tell you."

Giovanni, being a curious boy, was eager to learn what the little man had to say. "What can you tell me that is so special?" asked Giovanni.

Looking up at the small boy, Pepe said with a powerful voice, "Come with me, I will take you to a land with beautiful flowers where the days are filled with sunshine. At night stars, like diamonds, brighten the skies. You can run through the green forests, eat delicious sweet berries, and play all day long."

Filled with excitement, Giovanni begged, "Oh, please

Circa 1943, Stile Craft employees take a break. Among them are: Rose Beia, Mary D'Angelo, Toni Salamone, Marie Bertani, Becky _____, Mary Puricelli, and Tina Aceto.

take me there. Please! Please!"

"Just one more thing," cautioned Pepe, "If you come, you can never go home."

"You mean. . .you mean, I will never, ever see my mother again?" said little Giovanni with tears in his eyes. "My mother means more to me than all the beautiful flowers on earth, or all the sparkling stars that shine in the heavens,"

Louise Brusati and godchild Judy Marcallini picnic in Forest Park in 1948.

Miss Vismara and her sister Pierina Savio dare to ride a motorbike!

Girls' night out in the 1940s. From left to right: Tina Aceto, Marie Bertani, Sara Sciuto, Mary Contongi, Mary Monticelli, Eleanor Berra, Theresa Vago, Marie Lange, and Angeline Savoldi.

shouted Giovanni as he ran away.

Pepe mused, "I suppose it is true what these earthlings believe: *Il piu bel dono di Dio, é il cuore della mamma.* (God's most beautiful gift is a mother's heart.) ◆

Bella Bimba Pretty Doll

◆ My nonna, Theresa, always gave us wonderful advice. She never preached or scolded us. Instead, she told us traditional tales that ultimately taught us a lesson. I remember sitting around the coal stove on a cold December night and nonna narrated one of her favorite legends.

Shaw School's 1933 graduation day was a happy one for Grace Calcaterra.

There once was a silly couple who had a lovely, but not too bright daughter, Catarina, who was not married. Finally, her parents found a young man who agreed to be her husband. Her parents held a great wedding feast and invited all their friends and relatives. Everyone was happy until, right in the middle of dinner, there was no more wine to serve the guests. The father said to his daughter, "Go down to the cellar and bring up more wine."

The young bride obeyed and immediately opened the wine-barrel tap to fill the bottle. While she waited for the bottle to fill she thought: "I am so happy. When I have a daughter I'll name her *Bella Bimba* because she will be like a pretty doll. But suppose the gypsies come and steal her?" At this thought Catarina burst into tears as if her heart would break. Forgetting the tap was open, the wine ran all over the cellar floor.

The guests waited and waited for the bride but she was nowhere to be seen. Her father whispered to his wife, "Go down and see what has happened."

In the cellar, the mother found her daughter crying and asked,

"Catarina, why are you so sad?"

"Oh Mamma, what if we have a baby girl and the gypsies steal her?"

Her mother began to cry, "Oh my poor stolen granddaughter. Oh, my poor daughter." They both burst into tears.

In the meantime, the cellar was filling up with wine. The father announced to the guests, "They both must have fallen. I shall go and see."

He, too, went down to the cellar and found his wife and daughter crying like babies. "What in God's good earth has happened to you?"

"Oh, if you only knew," they cried.

"In no time our Catarina will have a beautiful baby girl and the gypsies will come and steal her," wailed the mother.

At that, all three began to wail. When they did not return the bridegroom went to see what was wrong.

Gloria and Rose Gambaro, and Sarah Italiano are anxious to get on the tennis court.

Circa 1926, Frances Caroselo, Grazia Monaco, and Carmela Carosello enjoy each other's company.

Below: Rose DeLurgio arrived in America in 1946 to prepare for her wedding.

Rose Ruggeri, Josie Brusati, and Ann Gualdoni enjoy a Fourth of July truck-ride picnic.

Hearing all the wailing he followed the sounds to his wife and her parents who were waist deep in wine. He begged his new wife to tell him what was the matter.

"Husband, we will have a daughter, *bella bimba*, and the gypsies will steal her away from us."

At first he thought it was a joke but when he saw they were serious he became very angry.

"I'm leaving. I never realized you were all so stupid. I'm not going to join a family of simpletons." And so he left and did not even look back.

He walked a long way until he arrived at the river. He saw a man trying to unload a boat full of chestnuts with a pitchfork. The man was frustrated because they kept falling out.

"Why don't you use a shovel," suggested the bridegroom.

Isabelle Mocca (kneeling left) picnics with her "Sewing Circle" friends who meet weekly and embroider for their trousseaus in 1937.

It's washday and Maria Griffero's sheets are as white as snow!

"Why bless you, I never thought to do that," replied the man.

The bridegroom smiled and thought to himself, "That's number one. He is even dumber than my wife's family."

Walking a little farther along the river he met a farmer watering his donkey with a spoon.

"I've been trying to give my animal a drink but it never seems to be enough for him."

"Why don't you lead him to the water and let him drink for himself?" asked the bridegroom.

"What a great idea, I never thought of that!"

"That's number two," sighed the bridegroom.

Later, as he continued walking, he came upon a woman on the top of a grape arbor holding out a clean, neatly pressed white shirt.

"What in the world are you doing, woman?"

"Oh, my husband died and Padre Pepe told me that he went up to heaven. I'm trying to send up his Sunday shirt so he will look his best for the Lord," answered the widow.

"That's three! Everyone in this town must be more stupid than my wife." And so he decided to go back home.

"On your mark, ready, set, go!" Frances Bandera, Jennie LaFerla, Marie Vago, Clementine Respi, and Adeline DiLiberto.

Hopefully, this young bridegroom learned:

Chi lascia la via vecchia per la nuova, sa quella che lascia ma non sa quella che trova! (He who takes the new path instead of the old knows what he leaves but not what will unfold!) ◆

Gioca Della Bottiglia
The Bottle Game

◆During the Great Depression money was hard to come by. Naturally, my parents could not afford to shower us kids with toys. However, we truly were rich beyond measure. We had a very creative grandmother. Our nonna often told my brother and me this story about a magical game.

Once there lived a king and queen who had two children. They loved their little prince and princess so much that they gave them anything they desired. There was no toy they didn't have. One would think this would make them very happy. But no, they were never satisfied and always complained about being bored. They would fret and pout all day.

Nonna Cristina Calcaterra looks forward to a new life in America.

This made the king and queen very sad. So the king sent messengers throughout the town asking everyone, "What toy can please my children?"

Anne Torretta is a bridesmaid in the early 1900s.

All the townspeople wanted to help their king so they all sent in suggestions, perhaps a doll that could walk and talk, or a kite with a long, brightly colored tail that could fly higher than the clouds, or maybe a top that can spin for hours. Sadly none of these toys pleased the little prince and princess.

One day Giovanni, a poor peasant lad, approached the king with this suggestion. "Why don't you simply teach your children to play the *gioca con la bottiglia.* It is a magical bottle game."

The king begged Giovanni to go to the palace and teach the little prince and princess.

Giovanni agreed and went with the king and taught the children this game. He placed a bottle in front of the royal prince and said, "You must stand tall and try to drop gold coins in the bottle. Whenever a coin goes in you must stop and make a wish. Every wish you make will come true—maybe not today or tomorrow, but if the wish is a good one for you it will be granted!"

The prince and his sister played *gioca con la bottiglia* for hours, clapping their hands and shouting with joy every time a coin fell into the bottle.

As my nonna told me the story she

Proud members of the "Margaretta Tennis Club" in the early 1900s. Identified in the second row, the second "R" is Ida Re.

would get a milk bottle and a few clothespins and demonstrate how the game was played. She was quick to tell us that we would not be using any coins and that the clothespins would do very well. She stressed that the most important part of the game was to make a wish as soon as the pin hit the target. And always she would say that everyone in life should wish and dream for beautiful things and if they are good for us they will materialize.

My grandmother and her repertoire have long since passed away. I often marvel at her simple philosophy which is so much like the words I once read: "We should hold fast to dreams lest the dreams die and our life will be as a broken-winged bird that cannot fly." ◆

Gloria Clavenna and Johanna Valone are dressed for a walk in the snow.

Gloria Clavenna, Johanna Valone, Marie Merlotti, Evelyn Nettemeyer, and a friend help deliver the Post *and* Star *papers in 1932.*

Adele Sarto rides with children on Shaw School's merry-go-round in 1937.

Leda DiBartolo and sister Linda wait for their friends to come out and play.

Adele Sarto and Shaw School's 1939 tennis players.

Circa 1935, Leda DiBartolo takes her first pony ride.

Andre il' Ferre Furba (Andre the Cunning Blacksmith)

◆ We never tired of sitting in our backyard, eating grapes from our vines and listening to our mamma entertain us with tall tales and fables she learned from her mother.

A long time ago in Malvaglio lived

a poor blacksmith who could never find any work. He and his family were so poor they were almost starving. One day Andre said to his wife, "I must go away to find work. There might be some need for a blacksmith in the city. Maybe then I'll get lucky."

So the next day Andre went to the large city of Milan. As he walked through the streets he shouted, "Who needs the help of a blacksmith?"

A wealthy merchant approached Andre saying "Can you shoe my horse? Can you make me a fine sword?" Andre answered with great confidence, "Of course I can do anything you ask. I do fine work and I expect to be well paid." Glad to receive the service the merchant paid Andre 25 gold pieces.

Andre was very happy. He thought, "I have enough money to buy a donkey." So off he went to the market place and bought a fine-looking donkey. Mounting the donkey, Andre started to ride home to his wife to bring her the good news.

From a distance Andre saw robbers coming toward him. He knew they were up to no good so he took 20 gold pieces and hid them under the donkey's bushy mane. The two robbers did as Andre feared. They seized him and took his five gold pieces. He begged them for mercy, crying, "I am only a poor blacksmith trying to keep

Photo Left: Saint Ambrose eighth graders in a 1947 Christmas Pageant.

Nonna Carmelina Gianino proudly walks with her grand-baby Joseph in her backyard.

from starving." Just then the donkey began to move quickly and the 20 hidden gold pieces fell to the ground.

Andre continued to wail, "Now you know my secret. My donkey has magical powers. He produces gold pieces for me."

Excitedly the robbers said, "Sell him to us. We will give you anything you ask."

Andre, being very cunning, said, "Oh good sirs, I don't think it's wise for you both to own the donkey, you will only fight over the gold. Why don't each of you give me 20 gold pieces and each take turns owning him."

The robbers agreed. Each paid Andre and they rode off into the night. Andre was very happy and very proud. He stopped at an inn and ate a fine dinner. In the meantime, the robbers came to the realization that they had been fooled. They hurried back to find Andre and to punish him for his deceit.

When Andre arrived home he knew the robbers would come after him. He told his wife, "If anyone comes asking for me, you are to tell them that you will send my dog to find me and he will give me the message."

The next day the robbers found Andre's home and asked his wife to

Dolores Miriani takes her godchild Karen Pozzo for a stroll.

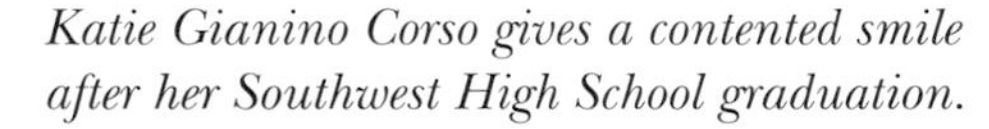

Katie Gianino Corso gives a contented smile after her Southwest High School graduation.

Rose and Gloria Gambaro share the task of mowing their lawn.

tell them Andre's whereabouts. His wife said, "Andre is somewhere in the meadow. I will send his dog to get him and tell him that you are here."

Speaking to the dog, Andre's wife said, "Go fetch your master and tell him there are some gentlemen who wish to see him."

"You think that dog can really find him?" said the robbers.

Andre's wife quickly replied, "Oh yes, he understands everything. He can actually talk."

Soon Andre returned and the robbers were very angry. They yelled at him for deceiving them about the donkey who made gold pieces. Andre calmly answered, "The poor animal's powers must have been confused with the change of masters."

The robbers then asked Andre if his dog really talked. "Of course," said Andre, "he understands everything."

"Well," said the robbers, "we will forget about the donkey if you will sell us the dog."

"Never," said Andre, "he is too valuable."

But, when the robbers offered him 50 gold pieces, Andre accepted.

They tied a chain around the dog's neck and they went their way. However, that evening they tried holding a conversation with the dog. Of course, the dog could not speak. He could only bark which made the robbers angrier than ever. They immediately returned to Andre's house to punish him for cheating them again. When they found Andre they tied him in a sack and told him they were going to throw him into the ocean.

Nonna Madelina Merlo, at left, visits with her relative from Italy.

They walked miles toward the sea but the sun was hot and the sack was very heavy. They stopped to rest under a tree and fell asleep. While they were sleeping Andre untied himself and crawled out of the sack. A shepherd was passing by with a large herd of sheep. Andre told him that the robbers were kidnapping him and were taking him to marry the king's daughter. Andre explained that he could not do that because he already had a wife.

The shepherd said, "Oh, how lucky you are! I wish I could marry the princess."

"That will be easy," replied Andre. "Just crawl in here."

The shepherd then opened the sack and took the cunning blacksmith's place.

When the robbers awoke they walked to the sea and threw in the sack. On their return they met Andre, and their mouths flew open in disbelief. Andre was standing in the middle of a very large herd of sheep.

Circa 1925, baby Gloria Gambaro enjoys her pet dog

Nettie Fontana, Lena Garagnani, and Frances Merlo go Christmas shopping.

Norma Garascia waits for friends, circa 1940s.

"Oh! We meet again," he said. "You will never believe how many sheep are in the sea. I just brought up these few and plan to go down and get some more. There are so many I could not count them. If you want to go and get some for yourselves I'll show you what to do. It is very simple. Each of you tie a stone around your neck so that you can go down very deep in the water. You will need large stones so that you can reach the deepest part."

The greedy robbers tied the stones around their necks, jumped into the sea and never came back up again. And Andre, the very sly blacksmith, ran home to his wife, where they lived happily to the end of their days. ◆

Rose Oldani prepares for an organ concert in St. Ambrose Church.

Netti Merlo and Lena Garagnani pose for a "sisters" photo, circa 1910.

Mamma Nunzia Russo and her daughter Annie Russo Gitto.

La Befana (The Good Witch)

Every nonna has told her grandchildren about *La Befana.* It is a classic Sicilian legend.

◆ *La Befana* was a very old woman who lived quietly alone, never involving herself in the affairs of others. She rarely had any visitors. But on one cold, wintry night she was visited by three richly dressed gentlemen who asked *La Befana* for help. They were seeking information about the birth of a special child. It was their desire to bring gifts to this infant but they had lost their way and needed someone to guide them.

Pina Garavaglia and Nettie Fontana enjoy apple picking.

Since *La Befana* was old and wise they wished her to accompany them and show them the way.

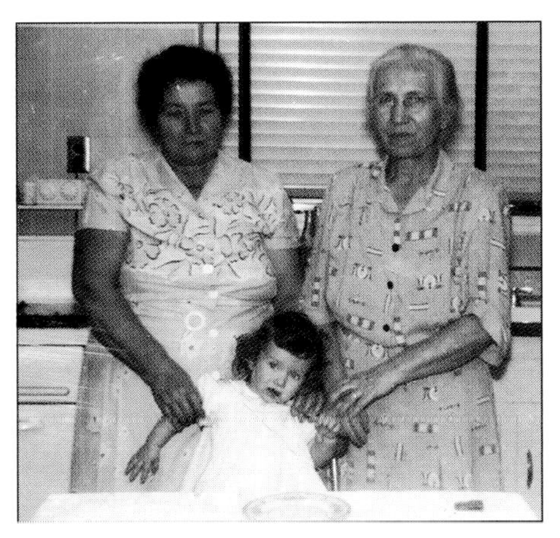

Nonnas Jennie Caputa and Felicia Garascia watch over Jeanette Caputa.

La Befana gave them many excuses: she was too old to travel, she was not feeling well, and she could not leave her nice home. Even after the visitors assured her that it was important for them to find this special baby and bring him wonderful gifts, *La Befana* still refused. The visitors left.

Later *La Befana* realized that her visitors were kings from foreign lands who were seeking the Christ child. She was overcome with guilt. Sadly, it was too late for her to join them. She traveled alone seeking to find the child. Whenever she came upon children she would give them gifts, always hoping that one day she would find baby Jesus.

So even today in our modern world, in every town, January 6th has become the Feast of the Epiphany (*La Befana* is a derivation of *epifania.*) On this day children receive gifts and their nonnas

Theresa Puricelli and friends enjoy coffee and delicious biscotti.

Fritz and Julia Garavaglia at Forest Park Highlands' dance. Circa 1935.

Friends from Saint Ambrose School pose for a photograph. Front row, left to right, are Carol Berra and Barbara Puricelli. Back row, left to right, are Shirley Puricelli and Margaret Frigo, circa 1940s.

relate the story of *La Befana* and how she gave gifts to children to make up for her unkindness to the Magi which kept her from finding the Christ child.

Customs surrounding the legend of *La Befana* differ from town to town. Many have all but disappeared, but in some regions January 6th is an important day to celebrate. Huge bonfires are built and women toss chestnuts into the fires. They believe chestnuts are a sign of fertility. If the smoke blows to the west the town will be blessed with an abundance of crops and the women of the town will be fertile.

The local young men carry an image of *La Befana* through the streets while strumming mandolins and singing:

Befana, Befana
We look for you each year.
You make our children happy
Whenever you appear.
Teach us to be kind
And generous to all
So that the Infant Babe
Will hear us when we call. ◆

Lena Denando and Fritz Garavaglia are fashionably dressed and ready to attend church.

Paulo, the Dreamer

◆ In the town of San Georgio lived Paulo and his wife, Angelina. Paulo was a good man but he was a dreamer, always thinking that good luck would certainly come his way. "Why should I work? One day a great fortune will be mine," he said to Angelina. Times were bad and they had little money, which caused Angelina to worry. But she held her head high and always obeyed her husband. She knew his dreams were foolish but she would not let the women in the town know how she felt. They often remarked, "Angelina, you should speak up to that foolish husband of yours. Tell him to go to work. He is just a lazy dreamer and too quick to do whatever silly idea comes into his head."

Nonna Carolina Lange celebrates her 94th birthday.

Angelina, an intelligent and patient woman, smiled and thought to herself, "One day he will learn and will change his ways."

Early one morning Paulo announced, "Angelina, I am going to Palermo. Today is the day of our great fortune. I am going into town to buy a lottery ticket. Keep your eye on the bridge at the end of town. If you see a carriage approaching it means that I have won. I shall ride home in style. When you see that carriage immediately throw out all of our old furniture. We shall buy everything new and live like kings!"

Serafina Mores walks with baby Virginia.

Angelina just smiled her usual smile. Hours later a stately carriage came into view. Obeying, Angelina threw out all the old furniture. When the carriage reached their hut the coachman helped Paulo from the carriage. He had fallen and broken his leg and the owner sent him home in his carriage!

After telling this tale my Nonna Nita would say, "Cara, life is not easy. We must always work for what we want. Remember: *Sogni come meglio vino si po fare aceto.* (Dreams like the best wine can turn to vinegar.)" ◆

Remembered Stories

◆ These stories I heard many times from my mother, Louise Oldani Chiodini, who came to St. Louis in 1927. My nonna, Angelina Colombo Oldani, who came from Cuggiono, relayed these stories in the oral tradition. This love of story telling, especially around the Sunday dinner table, has been passed onto the next generation.

The tales were moral lessons in faith, kindness, and sharing which, indeed, was the very manner in which they lived. My favorites were:

Circa 1920, the Garavaglia children patiently wait for their parents.

The Legend of the Robin

Christ was beaten, crowned with thorns, carried the cross, and was hanged on the cross to die. As He suffered, a small, simple brown bird flew around His head. Finally gathering the courage to relieve some of the suffering, it pulled at a single thorn, attempting to remove it. The struggle was long and difficult. When the thorn finally broke loose it pricked the bird's breast causing it to be covered with blood. For this great act of love, the color became permanent and the plain, drab-looking brown bird became the beautiful red-breasted robin.

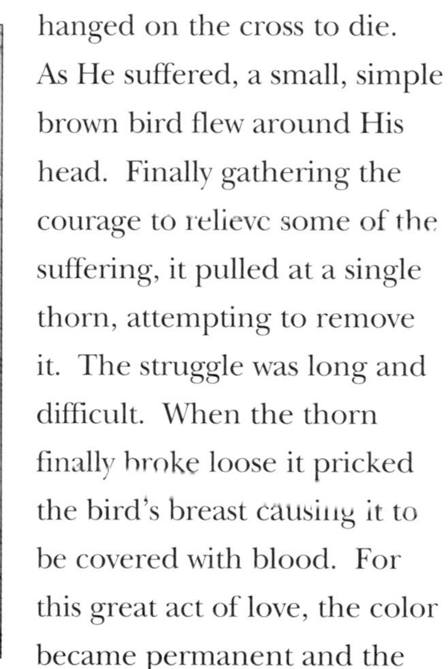

"Bunny" Longo, banjo instructor, waits for her cue to perform.

The Christmas Gift

Night came to Bethlehem, where in a stable, a baby boy was born. The father, who was a carpenter, put together a makeshift crib and lined it with straw. The child was wrapped and placed on this dry mattress when his first visitor, a fly, came by. The fly picked a dried flower from the straw and gently dropped it in the baby's hand. The baby's tiny fingers touched the fly causing it to light up and shine brightly.

Now on a summer's evening, if we look carefully into the darkness, we can see the firefly proudly showing the bright gift he received from the tiny Babe.

Nonnas Maria Salerno and Josephine Farretti take Mary Ann for a visit.

Ann Antinora, Mary Valenti, Carm and Jean Antinora, and Ann Palazzolo get ready for a 1940 "joy ride."

Dreams

One warm, sunny afternoon Frankie, the youngest son of my Uncle Joe, was playing in the alley behind his house. A car came speeding through the alley and sadly took little Frankie's life. When my uncle and aunt were preparing the clothing for his burial, they became very upset because they did not have new socks for him. They gave the mortician a pair of his older brother's socks, which of course, were too big.

For many days after the burial, Uncle Joe continually dreamed that little Frankie complained that he was having difficulty walking. Each morning Uncle Joe woke up so sad. Finally,

In the 1950s, Angelina Anselmo is joined in her backyard by her daughters for a photo that has been treasured by the family for many years.

Marian Yanni is the epitome of grace and charm in this 1935 graduation photo.

he told my zia that this recurring dream was upsetting him each and every morning. My aunt, a wise and loving woman, told my uncle that he must go out and buy a new pair of socks and give them to a young boy Frankie's age.

One Sunday morning my uncle came to our house and gave my brother, Dominic, a gift of a new pair of socks. From that night on my uncle slept peacefully. He never again had the upsetting dream of his beloved Frankie not being able to walk. ◆

Author Eleanore Berra Marfisi (in pigtails) with her sister and tennis partner, Mary Berra Enteman.

Nonna Ranzini and little Carolyn Ranzini bond together on nonna's front steps in the 1950s.

Nine-month-old Pauline Merlo was truly a bella bimba *(beautiful doll).*

The Aged Mother

◆ As I reflect on my childhood, I realize my mother taught us the greatest lessons right on our front porch.

Gloria Gianino, dressed in her finest, holds an Easter lily.

Mamma would sit with us ten children spinning tales as fast and as magically as her needles fashioned beautiful crocheted scarves. One particular tale I'll never forget was about an elderly lady and her selfish young children.

It seems that in her old age the mother had become a burden to her children. So it was decided that she should be taken across the mountain and left in a run-down asylum for the aged and infirm.

The children drew lots and it fell upon the youngest daughter to take their mother to the asylum. It was a long and tedious journey. Together they walked in silence. The mother was sad, but the daughter was determined!

The day was hot and the way was rugged and long. The daughter stopped to rest under a large cypress tree. As they sat down, the weary old mother looked up and reminisced, "I remember this spot. It's the same place I stopped when I took my mother to the same asylum you are taking me."

This caused the young daughter to ponder, "Oh my, maybe my children will one day do this to me when I grow old!" So, filled with remorse, she turned around and took their mother home and lovingly cared for her till the end of her days.

Then my sweet mother would sadly say in her native Calabrese: "*Nu madre crisciare dieci figli, ma dieci figli un campanu nu madre!* (A mother can raise ten children, but ten children cannot care for one mother!)" ◆

Circa 1950, Annie Gitto and Sarah Mae Sciuto sit outside Excel Ice Cream Parlor.

In the 1940s, Mary Barrale strikes a regal pose.

The 1949 sewing club celebrate. Left to right are Edith Raneri, Clem Garavaglia, Jennie Ravetta, and Marie Colombo.

Nonna and Her Home Remedies

Six sisters model their stunning, hand-crocheted, lace collars. Their married names are Marietta Berra, Giovanna Lange, Angelina Bottonelli, Cesarina Viglino, Vincensina Giudici, and Pierina Bianchi.

arly immigrant women were not only well-versed in the verbal arts, but also in the art of healing. They possessed a knowledge of incomprehensible secrets in the field of medicine.

For every ill, real or imaginary, there was a sure cure. If an immediate treatment eluded them, they never flinched because they knew: *Il tempo di malatie e necessita si vede il cuore.* (In times of illness one sees the heart.) Around every corner or across the street a *comare* (godmother) or a *bonamia* (good friend) would come to the rescue. Every woman had a special cure learned from her mother. They were truly medical legacies.

If anyone could be likened to Native-American shamans, it would be the early Italian-immigrant women. They, too, were miracle workers, doctors, and the forerunners of the modern medical profession.

These immigrants had little time and less money to run to the local doctor for every ailment. They immediately coped with whatever mishap or illness occurred and they often cited: *Mentre il medico studia, il malato muore.* (While the physician studies, the patient dies.)

Therefore, they practised their own cures.

Little Anthony Romano wears his dad's hat.

Raisins, Whiskey, and Parsley

◆ My Zio John had a great cure for arthritis. It was certainly unconventional. My Zia Anna would get so annoyed when he sang its praises. He simply soaked raisins in a jar of *grappa* (a rough, strong whiskey) for a whole month. Then every day he ate some raisins. He swore the pains not only subsided, they disappeared. Zio John said it was the raisins. However, Zia Anna said he didn't fool her. She would scream, "Its not the raisins. It's the *grappa* that makes you forget the pains."

Hers was a simpler method. Boil a bunch of fresh parsley with salted water. Then drink the juice three times a day while sitting in the sunlight. Enjoy the quiet of the day and the pains would disappear faster than gulping *grappa*! "My uncle said, *Simplice, si, meglio, mai!* (Simple, yes, better, never!)" ◆

Headaches

◆ Our neighbor Rosa had a special method for getting rid of headaches. She would take one small potato and cut two thin slices. Then she put a slice over each eye and sat on her rocker in a dark room.

Pauline Agosti (center, wearing a corsage) and friends celebrate Pauline's bridal shower.

Emilia Valloni Ravetta and friend are photographed before taking a summer stroll.

One afternoon my mother sent me to her house to stop my hiccoughs because Rosa was the great healer on our block. In those days we never locked our doors and I walked into her dimly lit room and two large white eyes stared back at me. I was just a kid and I thought some alien spirit was going to capture me and carry me away. I never knew if her headache was cured but I know my hiccoughs were gone.

Her more common method for curing a headache was to soak a cloth with vinegar, then wrap the cloth around one's forehead. For even quicker relief, she also recommended lying down in a darkened room. ◆

Earaches and Smoke

Remedies varied with each immigrant depending upon from which region in Italy she came. These methods may

Rose Oldani, music director, (center, third row, dark dress) with the Saint Ambrose Young Ladies' Choir in 1943.

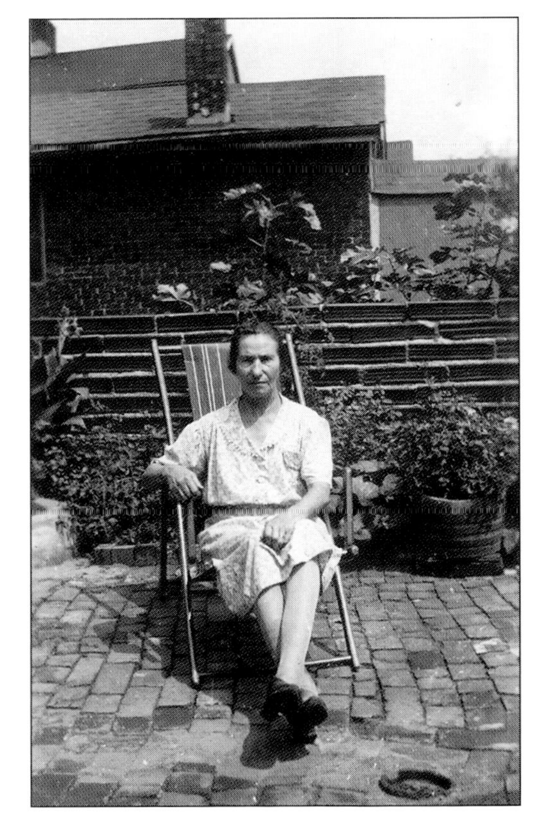

Louise Tapella says to relax is to refresh your soul!

seem totally unorthodox but cures and relief were often immediately apparent.

◆I remember my Nonna Gina's method for curing an earache. She claimed that every woman in her town practised this method and she swore by its success.

Nonna Marie Assunta Salamone patiently waits for her son to take her for a drive in the park. Circa 1940.

I was not quite convinced as I watched her roll a sheet of newspaper into a cone shape, warning me to *sta ferma* (stay still). She then placed the narrow end of the cone into my ear. My Zio Rico then blew smoke from his *toscano* (Italian cigar) into my ear. He repeated this several times as my nonna removed earwax and my pain was gone. My hearing was great again. I guess it was the heat of that horrible-smelling *toscano* smoke that did the trick.

However successful, there was always another *amica* (friend) who thought her method was better. One was to simply pour several drops of heated olive oil into the ear and the results would be the same: loosening earwax. ◆

Bruises and Infections

◆When we were kids, we always rode our scooters on the sidewalk. My little brother invariably fell and scraped his knees. My mother, ever ready to take care of all our bruises, always kept a piece of moldy bread, just in case. She would carefully place it over my brother's knee and then wrap a cloth around it. It healed in no time. In those days none of us ever heard the word "penicillin." I guess my unschooled, immigrant mother was really far ahead of the times. She discovered the power of penicillin before members of the medical profession.

Natalina Carolli's mother crocheted her exquisite collar.

Another method for checking infections was to make a paste of milk and sugar. After applying it to the sore, it was wrapped with a white cloth. This was repeated until the infection was gone. ◆

Garlic

The remedy of remedies in the Italian-American pharmacopeia was, undisputedly, garlic. Our nonnas were not alone in this belief. As early as the first century Pliny the Elder, the famous Roman encyclopedist, spoke of the power of garlic to combat snakebites. Other ancient writers wrote about garlic's superior healing qualities, believing that the powers were strictly magical.

The legend of the power of garlic was not lost on Italian-American caregivers. They were convinced that a pouch filled with garlic cloves worn around the neck was capable of multiple cures which included chest colds, sore throats, relieving worms, and clearing hoarseness. There is certainly, no doubt, that this method will also ward off friends, relatives, and even enemies.

"Nonnie" Marietta Berra and daughter Mary and grandson David Shaw.

Toothaches

◆We rarely went to the doctor unless we had something serious. And if we had a toothache any woman in the neighborhood could offer an immediate remedy. I don't think we ever went to the dentist. My Nonna Pia would simply spread the white of an egg on a small cloth. Then she folded the cloth carefully over the egg white and applied it to the swollen gums. This was repeated until the swelling went down. It was remarkable. I can't really say what did the trick. Maybe the protein in the egg was the secret. We kids didn't care about the rationale behind the cure; we were only glad it didn't hurt anymore! ◆

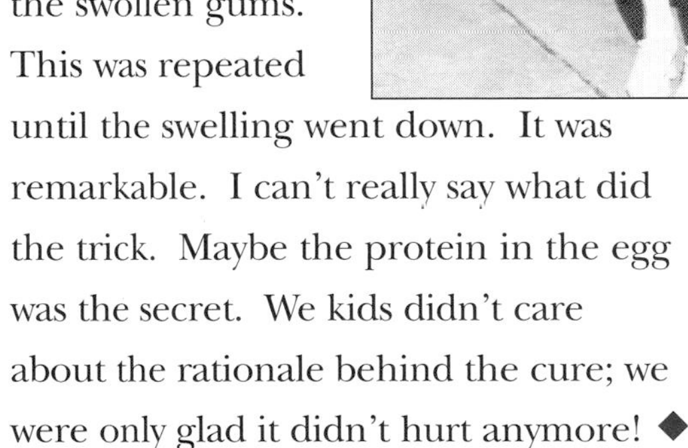

Dorothy Ronzio receives her nurse's cap in 1944.

Warts

◆ Faustina, my mother's friend, knew all the secrets of how to cure just about anything. Her specialty was warts. She would slice a fresh eggplant and wrap it around the wart. She then tied a cloth around it to keep it in place. This was one method. The other was, in my childish mind, weird!

Baby Cosima is lovingly held by her Nonna Cosima Porcaro, circa 1915.

Faustina cut a potato in half and then immediately rubbed it over the wart. She buried the potato in her backyard. In her words we had to "*aspettare la luna* (wait for the moon)." We were to look for a full moon, dig up the potato, and the wart would be gone!

Louise Airoldi and her mother enjoy an afternoon in their backyard.

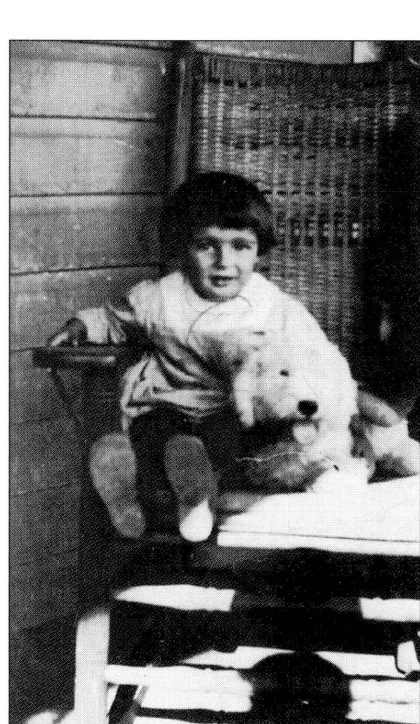

Angeline Pozzo in 1918 hugs her pet dog.

Sties

Faustina's cure for sties made my hair stand straight up. She took a large butcher knife in hand and leaned over me. That blade was so big and shiny, I thought I was going to be butchered. Instead, Faustina told me to sit still as she placed the cold blade over my sty. In a few days it was gone. I'm not sure whether Faustina's cure was magical or if I scared the sty away! ◆

Mushrooms

◆ When my Zia Gina decided it was time to teach my cousin Ann the secret of mushrooms, the first lesson was where she could find them growing. This was critical because she did not want anyone else to find her cache. Mushrooms were valuable, not only because they tasted good, but also, according to my zia, they were very important in building strong bones.

After Zia Gina and Ann returned home with mushrooms my cousin learned the BIG secret. Because some

Leonarda Gandolfo, at right, celebrates her 98th birthday.

Three stately women in 1900 – Jennie, Giovanna, and Guiseppina Mazzuca – preserve this memory for future generations.

mushrooms were poisonous you had to be extremely careful. Before you could even think of eating them you should boil them with a silver half-dollar. If the coin turns black they are poisonous. Do not eat them!

So my cousin Ann was entrusted with this great test. When my Zia asked, "Did you put in the fifty-cent piece?"

She answered, "I couldn't find one so I put in a quarter, two dimes, and a nickel." Obviously Ann failed the mushroom test! She still laughs about it to this day. ◆

Salt

The early Romans worshipped salt, claiming it possessed many powers. It was often called "the magic white sand." Its importance can readily be seen in the words of Christ when He speaks to each of us saying: "You are the salt of the earth." But to the Italian immigrant salt also had healing powers!

Theresa Puricelli, a gracious woman, strikes a pensive pose, circa 1915.

Rose Oldani and Marie Ronzio have a lawn picnic with children Marie and Louis.

Mary Coco Oehler waves to her friends.

Sore Throat

◆ Nonna's cure for a sore throat was a novel one. She poured one cup of salt in a frying pan and heated it until it was very hot. The heated salt was poured on a large piece of cloth – usually cut from a flour sack. The cloth with the salt was wrapped around the sore throat.

Another medical breakthrough for the early immigrant woman. ◆

Colds

◆ The following treatment for colds was a popular one. Ladies from the towns of Palermo in the south and Cuggione in the north swore by its success.

Carefully pour one cup of wine into a small saucepan. Add a half cup of sugar, then heat to a boil. You may add a few cloves to the mixture. Drink this mixture as hot as possible. Then go right to bed and cover up with a blanket. Remain under the covers until perspiration stops. Your cold will not only be gone, you may not even remember you had a cold. ◆

Getting ready to catch the "big one" before it gets away are Florence Re, Anna Berra, and Rose Colombo in the 1940s.

Fun in the backyard with Nonna Lena Brusatti, Marie Bertani, and Irene Brusatti.

Connie DeMartino enjoys the beautiful wildflowers.

Bee Stings

◆ Whenever any of us children got a bee sting my mother was quick to act. She ran to the kitchen and grabbed a knife. The first time she did this I almost fainted! Believing I was going to get cut really scared me.

To my relief she placed the edge of the knife blade over the sting area and held it there for three minutes. Then she made a baking soda paste by adding a few drops of water to a tablespoon of baking soda. My mother then applied the paste over the sting. She made sure I kept this paste on for an hour, which to my child's mind seemed like an eternity. But my wise mother, in her simple way, made my pain go away. ◆

Adriana and Domenica Fazio spend a pleasant afternoon together.

Boils

◆ My feisty Nonna Carmelina had a novel way of curing boils. She would place a lighted candle under a glass. Then she would place the glass over the boil. When the oxygen burned out, a vacuum was created and the boil was drawn out.

Now that I am in college and a science major, it astounds me that nonna was actually practising the laws of physics. I had to cram my head with Gaylussac's Theory of the Dependence of Volume and Temperature - my nonna just used common sense. So much for formal education. ◆

Cloves

The Romans gave the clove its name, *clavus,* because it was shaped like a nail. They believed it made the breath sweet and even relieved vomiting. However, my mother always said, "Keep a clove on your aching tooth and the pain will soon be gone."

Nonna Carolina Sasso and children arrive in Saint Louis in 1920.

Nonna Grazia Monaco was a midwife and a healer in Italy. When she came to America she only practised her art when friends sought her help. When we were growing up she often spoke of various cures, among them were the following:

Colic Cures

◆ To cure a colicky baby, make a weak tea with water and bay leaf. Add a little sugar and give it to the baby as often as needed.

Young Disolina Bagatti was soon to arrive in America for her wedding, circa 1900.

Josephine Berra Shaw shyly smiles at the photographer.

Sprained Ankle or Wrist

Beat one egg white with some cream of tartar or salt until peaks form. Immediately place the egg whites on the sprained area and wrap it with gauze or a large dishcloth. Leave it on overnight and the swelling will be gone the next day. ◆

Nonna Anna Mugavero poses for a photo to send to her family in Italy after she became a U.S. citizen.

Aches and Pains

◆ We had a neighbor who constantly moaned about aches and pains. My wise mother would gently remind her to ignore them. "Just sing," she would say, "and they will go away." Together they would spontaneously sing verses of *Canzone di Picchio* (The Woodpecker's Song). She forgot her pains but my father claimed their singing gave him a pain! ◆

Cure a Rash

◆ Mix "some" sulfur and salt. Apply it to the rash. The next day the rash will be gone. ◆

Angeline Coco, Anna George, Mary Caponi, and Mrs. Lyle have fun celebrating their birthdays in the 1950s.

Olive Oil

◆ A teaspoon of olive oil rubbed gently along the spine of an infant will help the baby's bowel movements. ◆

Wrinkles

◆ I learned some wild cures from my mother's sister, Josepina. We called her Zia Pina. She claimed that no woman should tolerate having wrinkles. Her cure was to melt white candles under a gentle heat until you have "just enough." She never explained how much "just enough" was. You were to put this on your face twice a day. When I asked, "Zia, how long should I keep it on?" She answered with all honesty, "Just long enough!" After the application you were to wash your face with warm water and your wrinkles would disappear. ◆

Lemons

Rose Fontana Kelso gets ready to toss her ball.

◆ For Beautiful Skin:

In a pint of milk squeeze the juice of a lemon. Apply it to the face every night. Rinse it off in the morning with warm water. The lemon will instantly give your skin a clear beauty.

For Inflammatory Arthritis:

Eating a lemon everyday is a sure cure for arthritis. To the early pioneer immigrant the juice of lemons had multiple uses including the removal of ink stains, iron, rust, and even freckles! ◆

It is easy to understand why these home-made remedies have not disappeared with the passing of these wonderful healers. If one could penetrate the core of today's miracle drugs, one might discover the essence of some of nonna's ingredients scientifically hidden in the pills of modern medicine.

Francesca Vago and Maria dress in their finest for a mother-daughter photo, circa 1920.

We do not encourage, nor do we suggest, that these remedies be tried. They are simply a legacy left to us by the loving, ever so creative, valiant, immigrant-Italian women.

We have only scratched the surface of our efforts to unearth these remedies. We invite you to think of your own childhood and all the special remedies your mother practised on you.

Superstitions: Shadows of Truth

Mamma Mugavero and daughters Marie (left) and Francesca (right) were certainly women of style, circa 1923.

uperstition is inherent in all cultures. It is mirrored in the history of man. Nowhere is this more apparent than in the beliefs and practices of early women immigrants.

Superstitions were and continue to be intrinsic in their nature and perhaps can never be wholly extricated.

We have all grown up with many superstitions. In this, our modern age, we may scoff but we must remember how many brides would not think of getting married without "something old, something new. . ." We all remember "Don't open the umbrella in the house," or "Never walk under a ladder."

Many of these strange and sometimes eerie practices were so immutable, they have not been lost in the antiquity of time. It is important to understand that superstitions were impelled by a will to survive. Early Italian immigrants, not unlike any immigrant, found themselves in an alien world far from the comfort zones of their homeland. They had little money, large families, and an obvious language barrier. They had no easy access to psychologists, counselors, or even medical doctors.

Mary Denando Berra and Josie Marcallini are ready for a drive in the country in 1943.

Therefore, their tales of the old country, their home remedies, proverbs, and especially their superstitious practices, learned from their nonnas, provided them with a degree of comfort, security, and peace of mind.

The Witch

We all, at one time or another, have heard stories and can relate in some detail strange happenings involving weird superstitions. When we hear the term "witch" we easily conjure up a number of visual impressions . . . an old woman with a wart on her nose, riding on a broomstick, clad in a black robe, and wearing a pointed hat.

Left to right: Mary Noe, Mary Fontana, Angela Zarinelli, Angela Mazzola, and Katie Rossi raise funds at a charity car wash in the late 1940s.

But to Italian old-timers a witch was entirely different. She was a normal looking female, called a *strega* or a *stria*, who was born with evil powers. One of her most malevolent was the *malocchio* (evil eye).

The *strega* had this uncanny ability to inflict injury simply by staring at the victim with the evil eye. Then, voila, an instant headache or even something worse. It is well to keep in mind that when they fell ill, the early immigrants could not afford to go to a doctor. Therefore, they practised methods learned from their mammas on how to cope with misfortune and bad luck.

So for every *strega* that was romping about, there was the *fattachiara* (loosely translated – one who makes clear or clears up). She was the antithesis of the *strega*. She performed various rituals to remove the evil spells. She even taught other women her secrets so they would not be lost in time.

Back row, left to right: Mary Spezia, Cella Grassi, Josephine Calcaterra, and Rose Grassi. Front row, left to right: Norma Magnano, Anna Jo Grassi, and Rose Marie Berra on her First Communion day.

The Headache

The *fattachiara* cured a headache especially if it was the result of a *strega* giving the person the *malocchio.* This was a simple procedure:

First, dip the thumb into a spoonful of olive oil. Make a sign of the cross on the forehead of the afflicted person. Then, again, dip the thumb in the oil. Let a small drop of oil drop in the water and while doing this recite: *In nomine padre, figlio, spirito santo pensa la beata Virgine. Due occhi fanso offeso porta via questo male.* (In the name of the Father, Son, and Holy Spirit. Think of the blessed Virgin. Two eyes have offended me. Take away this curse.)

Giovanina Monti (at far right), caterer, and her servers.

Caterina Brusatti, Senora Salemie, and Angelina Marino are ready for a party at the Palma Augusta Club, circa 1938.

Lost Lover

The *fattachiara* also knew how to regain the affections of a lost lover or a husband who might be contemplating infidelity. It was a simple chant to accompany the following.

One must acquire a piece of the loved one's clothing and while holding it over a flame say:

Quando questo pezzo di materiale com-
incia bruciare
Fa il cuore del mia amore
Ritorni con mille volte
L'amore che io perduta.
(As the soul begins to burn
So will the heart of my lover
And it will return a thousand times
The love that I have lost.)

Another method to regain or keep a husband's love is to obtain a small cloth bag containing salt, ground red rose petals, and pieces of blue string. Slip these in the husband's pocket or sew them in the lining of his jacket. Every time he leaves the house he will not stay away for long. He will yearn to return to his true love and never be unfaithful again.

Grace and baby brother Nick Belfiglio pose for a studio picture in 1930.

Whistling Girls

◆ My favorite superstition was learned from my mother. She believed: "Girls should never whistle because it will make the Blessed Virgin cry!" As a kid my brother taught me to whistle. No doubt, I must have driven my mother wild and repeating her advice was her method of curing me from whistling. When I questioned, "Does the Virgin cry when boys whistle?" Her only comment was, "Girls, only girls, should not whistle!" ◆

Circa 1920, Louise Brusati Henneke, Mary Berra Franceschi, and Ida Rolfi dress in their Sunday best.

Eda Grassi enjoys a delightful afternoon with her beautiful baby Linda.

Amulets

Amulets offered absolute protection from the evil eye. The most popular is the *corno* (horn), shaped like a horn. Amulets were used to fascinate and focus the person who was determined to give someone the *malocchio.* A person's first glance was said to be the most dangerous. So if somebody threatens harm it is crucial that the first look be redirected onto the *corno.* The *corno* then captures the first glance and protects the intended victim. It is worn conspicuously so the amulet is often bright gold or ornamented with jewels. These will certainly trap the *malocchio's* first glance and deflect any evil or demonic power.

Mary Coco and sister Angelina start for a stroll around the neighborhood in 1950.

Superstitions are certainly not always rational, but to the early Italian-immigrant women they are traditional. And tradition is an enormous magnifier. It is amazing how a thing grows in the human imagination when fear for loved ones, spiritualism, and all that lies in the human heart is there to encourage it.

Exploring the superstitions of Italian women and their customs is surprisingly not always irrational, rather, it is more often ethnic, or humorous and curious to the modern mind.

Salt

◆ My six-year-old son, Johnny, spilled salt while sitting at the table with his grandmother. Nonna Russo immediately told him to throw the salt over his shoulder. He looked at her with a quizzical look and said, "Are you sure nonna?" She said "Yes, hurry or you will have bad luck." My son picked up the entire salt shaker and threw it over his shoulder! So much for good luck! ◆

What could be more fun than a swim at Forest Park Highlands' Pool.

The Owl Hoots

As children we were told that owls hooting at night was a bad omen. It is doubtful that we ever heard or saw an owl flying free in our neighborhood. Perhaps it was a belief handed down from Roman ancestors that if one hears the hoot of an owl it was the sign of death! Even Shakespeare spoke of the death of Julius Caesar: "Yesterday, the bird of night did sit even at noon day, up on the marketplace, hooting and shrieking." Could Shakespeare be wrong?

Keep The Lightning Out

◆ Nonna Anna Mutolo Torpea, from Palermo, Sicily, with all the other ladies in the neighborhood would pull down all the shades and cover mirrors with sheets and towels when there was a storm. She believed this would keep lightning from getting through and bouncing around the house, hitting the mirror, and inflicting us with bad luck. ◆

Rose and Gloria Fontana enjoy a ride on the swing.

Maria Zarinelli Griffero and daughter Emilia pose with a garden basket in 1915.

Mary Kolafa and son Vince take an early spring morning stroll.

Boy or Girl?

The ever-wise nonna was able to predict the sex of an unborn child long before ultra-sound imaging. If a soon-to-be mother wished to know the sex of her baby, nonna would simply take a string, about eight inches in length, and attach a button to it. She would suspend it over the expectant mother's right hand. If it swung in a circular motion the baby was a girl. If it went straight back and forth the baby was a boy.

Theresa Belfiglio and daughter Grace's picture was taken for Theresa's mother who had remained in Italy.

Beautiful Baby

◆One day while taking a walk with my little baby girl, my neighbor stopped me with a warning. "Eda," she said, "If anyone stops you and tells you that your little Angela is beautiful,

In the 1950s, Nonna Gina Luigia Colombo gives granddaughter Marie Merlotti advice for a happy life!

Johanna Savio sports her new bike in 1946.

hurry home and pin a ribbon on her. The ribbon must be red to stop the *malocchio.* The stranger may be a *strega* and wishes harm to your baby simply because she is jealous of you for having such a beautiful child!"

She made me so nervous I was pinning red ribbons all over the house! When I told my nonna about this she laughed. I felt relieved until she said, "No, no, just make the *cornu* then Angela will be protected." (The horn-like *cornu* sign is made by extending your index and little finger.) I soon learned to smile rather than to put their advice into action. ◆

Enrichetta Ruggeri and Theresa Colombo (at right) celebrate Joanna Colombo's graduation from nursing school.

Evil Peacocks

Many believed having birds in the house would bring bad luck. Never keep peacock feathers in your home because they carry the evil eye on them.

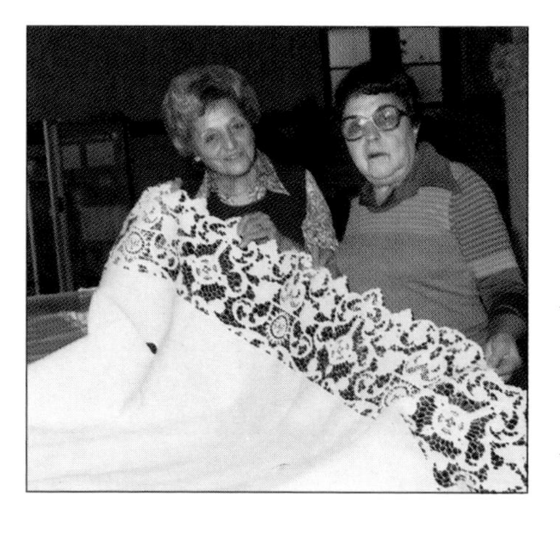

Anita Gualdoni and Ann Cassani prepare Saint Joseph's Altar cloths.

In 1923, Grace Calcaterra takes a pony ride around the Hill.

Black Cats

It was also a bad omen to have a black cat cross one's path. To have one enter the house was a sure sign of impending disaster.

Nightmares

Nightmares were generally interpreted as bad omens. Dreaming of teeth or muddy water was a sign of death. Dreaming of babies forecast good things to come.

Saint Anthony

One early spring morn, when the air was warm and I was happy to be alive, my world came apart. I looked down and saw that I had lost my wedding band. Never had I removed the ring from my finger. I have worn it since the day that we were married, thirty years ago. Totally devastated, I called my mother for consolation. She immediately began to scold me, "Why are you wasting your time crying? Pray to Saint Anthony and he will find your ring. Just say what my mother

The Ladies' Society gets ready for its annual pilgrimage to sites such as the missionary retreat house in Starkenburg, Missouri.

taught me. . .*Sant Antonio fa me la grazia* (Saint Anthony give me the grace)."

"But mom," I moaned, "I don't pray in Italian."

Josephine Devoti enjoys a walk in the country in 1940.

She always had an answer. "Well just say, Saint Anthony, in this hour shine forth and show thy power."

However, in spite of my prayer, I could not locate the ring. My mother ignored my disbelief. After many months, the seasons rolled on. Suddenly it was autumn. Time to rake leaves and get the garden ready for a winter's sleep. Voila! There among the leaves was my ring!

I cannot say that my mother and her devotion to Saint Anthony was pure, unadulterated faith or simply another of her many supersti- tions. However, I must admit that in spite of the fact that I claim not to be superstitious, I often find myself calling upon Saint Anthony.

La Famiglia

◆ My grandmother often told stories about the dead and how important it was that they are never forgotten. In my childish mind I feared that they would come back in the dark of night to haunt me and maybe even carry me away! But my Nonna Sunta always assured me that would never happen because they are *nostra famiglia* (our family). "Just because they are no longer on this earth doesn't mean they have forgotten us.

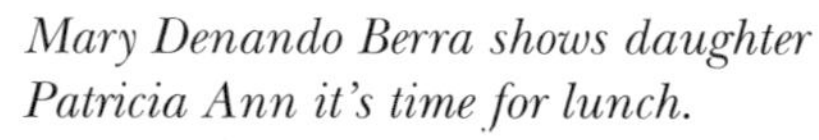

Mary Denando Berra shows daughter Patricia Ann it's time for lunch.

So we must never, never forget them."

Nonna Sunta would then take out all the old pictures and tell stories about each one. . .the uncle who fought in the war. . .the cousin who raised goats and sold their milk. . .the little nephew who went to heaven too soon. When she came across the picture of her father playing the accordion at weddings, she always smiled.

November 2nd, All Souls Day, was a time of special feasts. It was also a day of surprises: I would find candy, fruit, and little toys at the foot of my bed. Nonna sat beside me and explained that these gifts were given in the name of our relatives who were no longer with us. ◆

Wedding Superstitions

Superstitions revolving around weddings are still prevalent in Italian-American communities. Among them are:

Throughout the ages almonds were revered as blessings for marriages. Brides, even today, distribute almonds at their wedding feasts. They are

Margherita Garavaglia and her sister Louise leave Italy and travel to America in 1929.

Lena Montani, Albina Berra, Linda Montani, and Ann Macchi (kneeling) meet for a game in the park.

believed to foster a fruitful union. If it rained on a wedding day it was considered lucky. When I questioned this I was told, "It is harder to untie a wet knot."

A diamond engagement ring has long become an integral symbol to the young Italian future bride. As early as 860 A.D. Pope Nicholas I decreed that the engagement ring was a required statement of nuptial intent. The tradition of the "diamond" engagement ring comes from the 15th century Venetians. Since the diamond is the hardest and most enduring substance in nature it follows that the engagement and marriage will last forever.

Judy Piantanida Marcallini looks to be very deep in prayer for her First Communion photo.

Mary Minnella, a 1951 bridal attendant.

Grace Giuffrida and her young cousins Pina and Tony Coco, circa 1915.

The Italian bride would never think of walking down the aisle without carrying flowers. Perhaps this may have its roots from ancient Romans who believed that carrying strong-smelling herbs would ward off evil spirits.

It was not unusual in the early Italian-immigrant family to arrange the meeting of potential husbands for their daughters. In more than one instance the groom saw his bride for the first time on the day of their wedding. The marriage of an unattractive daughter was often arranged between the families. To prevent the surprised groom from changing his mind and leaving the bride at the altar, the bride's face was covered with the wedding veil only to be removed after the vows were made. Perhaps this custom dates back to Biblical times with the marriage of Jacob to Leah (the older sister) when Jacob thought he was marrying Rachel, the lovely young sister whom he loved.

Marianna Pona, back row second from right, and World War II women defense workers pause for the photographer.

◆ When I got married my mother, who was born in Palermo, insisted I have a little flower girl drop rose petals when she walked up the aisle before me. Mamma claimed it was to ward off evil spirits and would assure my having children. ◆

◆ When a bride leaves her home on her wedding day, a relative breaks a dish as the bride steps out of the door. This custom symbolizes that she "breaks" with her old home to start a new one with her husband. ◆

The Italian Kitchen

The Italian kitchen is one place where many superstitions are manifest.

◆ My grandmother always said, "What falls to the floor, comes to the door."

If a fork accidentally falls on the floor, a man will knock on your door. A spoon means a woman but, God forbid, if a knife falls on the floor someone will come in and bring bad luck. ◆

Angie Anselmo (far left) and friends enjoy a picnic.

Frances Grana and Ann Cipolla prepare for a brisk winter walk.

◆ We never place bread upside down on the table. My mother always made us turn it over because it was considered inauspicious. I'm sure she did this because she looked upon it as the bread of life. Moreover, bread was always broken, never sliced. We were taught that bread was a gift from God and it would be wrong to cut it. And if by chance, one of us was lucky enough to get the heel of the bread, good luck was sure to come. ◆

On the feast of Saint Joseph bread was blessed. Many families took tiny pieces of the blessed bread and wrapped them around a coin. Then they would place them on the sills of each window in the home. This talisman ensured the family would never go hungry nor live without sufficient funds. This practice is continued today simply because it is symbolic.

Angie, Josephine, and Frances Anselmo are lovely bridal attendants.

Louise Chiodini (photo center) celebrates a birthday with her grandchildren.

Dolores Corolli splashes in her Nonna Pozzo's backyard pond.

Taking a loaf of bread and a box of salt to a friend who has moved into another home remains a current tradition. The bread and the salt are to be stored in the pantry for *buona fortuna* (good luck) so that the families may never go hungry and may never be without salt which represents the salt of the earth . . . health and happiness.

If a woman's apron comes untied by itself and falls off while she is working in the kitchen, this is a sure sign that someone is thinking of her. Some believe that it really means her sweetheart is having romantic thoughts about her that very moment.

When salt and sugar are accidentally mixed up, it is believed to be an omen of good news to come.

Josephine Anselmo and Sandy and Cheryl Falduti go wading.

Nonna Gina Valloni picks vegetables from her garden.

Gold Earrings

Every little girl born in Sicily in my mother's hometown wore earrings. Their ears were pierced when they were infants. It was done, according to my mother, not out of a sense of style but rather because of a very strong superstition. It was believed and perpetrated that gold near the eyes would always ensure keen vision and healthy eyes.

Catherine Tedesco and daughter Beverly enjoy a walk in the park.

Friends enjoy Shaw's Garden's lily pond.

Mary Valenti shows promise as a great athlete, even as a child. Photo circa 1920.

Three sisters —Mary Faith, Janet, and Bernadette Riganti— enjoy a good time together in the 1950s.

"If a woman is in the family way (pregnant) and she craves a certain food and is not satisfied, the baby will have a birthmark resembling the food she craved."

Biagia Pietro Burgo is holding one of her intricately embroidered pillow cases. She was 92 years old in this photo.

The Riganti sisters enjoy having their picture taken, circa 1948.

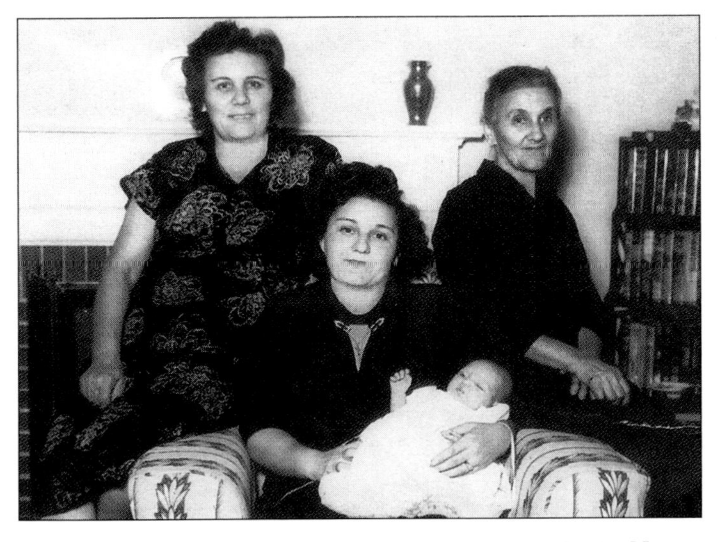

Four generations celebrate: baby Linda, mother Mary Savio, Nonna Jenny Ruggeroli, and great grandmother Josephine Ruggeri.

Shadows of Truth

Enjoying a cappuccino at our local coffee shop was always a trip down memory lane. We second-generation daughters of Italian immigrants often get together, if only to recall how great it was growing up in our special Italian community.

Advice we each received from our mothers was always a great topic. Mammas had strong beliefs on every phase and facet of life. However sincere their admonitions, we "modern Americans" found them totally illogical and laughed at the mention of each! We could almost hear our mothers saying,

"I learned this from my nonna so I know it must be true." Included in their prosaic wisdom are:

- Don't ever cross your eyes, even in fun; they will freeze and you will be cross-eyed for the rest of your life.

- Remember that when you have a baby never, never keep a cat near the infant, especially when the baby is sleeping. The cat will steal the baby's breath and the baby might die.

- Do not sleep with your windows open. The night air is bad. . .malaria! It brings sickness into the house.

Jennie LaFerla, Rose Venegoni, Caroline Puricelli, and Emilia Valloni meet for a friendly visit in 1950.

Nata Torno takes pride in her decorated altar.

Stephanie Venegoni (second from right) and her bathing beauty friends in the 1930s.

Pineta Giambelli (left) and Emilia Garanzini watch over Fred Vonogoni and Carol Stelzer in 1950.

Nonna Consolino (left) and Nonna Carmela LoCastro share babysitting of the LoCastro twins.

Mamma Marietta Carnaghi holds baby Julia for the camera in 1924.

- Never, but never go out alone at night when there is a full moon. The light of the moon brings out all the lunatics and they will hurt you.

- Never wear pearls. They are tears congealed and will bring bad luck.

- Never start a new job, begin a trip, or conduct business on Friday.

Mary Berra, Mary Enteman, and Patricia Berra enjoy the park, circa 1945.

Angeline Macchi and Katie Rancilio, school friends, share a genial moment, circa 1920s.

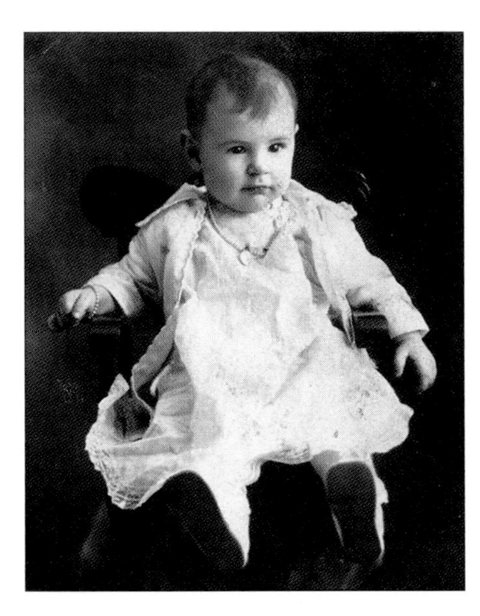

Eleanore Berra's first studio photo.

- If two items are overlapped on a table forming a cross, they should be uncrossed immediately while making the sign of the cross.

- On New Year's Eve, if an individual is holding money in his hand or eating something green when the clock strikes midnight, he will be guaranteed good fortune in the coming year.

- Weddings should never take place in May or August or during the seasons of Lent or Advent. May is a month that is reserved for veneration of the Blessed Mother and to marry in August will bring bad luck and sickness to the couple.

Below: Lena and John Carnaghi don costumes for a World War I play.

Four friends, left to right: Frances Fassi, Gina Garanzini, Louise Viola, and Adele Garagiola.

Colleen Mazzola (left) and Helen Marino are warmly dressed in a winter scene.

- Never point your finger at anyone. Your four fingers will point back at you and you will be the one who is guilty.

- Wear a garland of rosemary around your neck. It will make your memory better.

- If you give a lock of hair to a man it is an act of "surrender." It means you entrust to him your life and your love.

Maria Simione (left) and friend Rosalie enjoy their rose garden.

• If a *strega* gets a single strand of your hair she could cast a spell and bewitch you.

• Never fear a big storm with lightning and thunder. Simply take a piece of blessed palm, light it, and hold it out towards the door. The storm will soon subside.

• Always wear your new clothes to church first. God deserves the best.

• When a loved one is leaving on a trip or will be away from you for an extended time, cross him/her on the forehead with holy water and say, "*Aqua Santa che ti bagna, Jesu Christo ti compania dove va dove si Jesu Christi compangnia ti.* (I bless you with Holy water. Jesus Christ accompany you where you are, where you will be. Jesus Christ be your companion.)"

Ann Cipolla teaches Angela Marino how to mail a letter.

Fannie and Mary Berra model their new spring dresses, circa 1950.

Angeline Macchi dressed in winter attire, circa 1920.

- If a woman is in the family way (pregnant) and she craves a certain food and is not satisfied, the baby will have a birthmark resembling the food she craved.

- When a cat washes its face it will surely rain the next day.

- To dream of clear water is a sign that good luck is on the way. But to dream of muddy water means whatever you plan the next day will go wrong.

Serafina Garavaglia (left) and school friends, circa 1920.

Angelina Torretta, Hill childrens storyteller.

Nonnas Gina Valloni (left) and Nata Torno are proud to show off grand-daughter Agnes Torno.

- While gold and silver are shiny and beautiful, to dream of them means "no good" is coming.

- If you think someone may wish you harm, simply look at them and say with all your heart: *Dio ti Benedica* (God bless you) and you will be turning evil into good.

The Clarion *staff are busy preparing the paper in this 1948 photo. This newsletter was sent to servicemen during and after WWII.*

Helen Marino and friends plan a special evening together, circa 1945.

Fritz Garavaglia sports her beautiful coat.

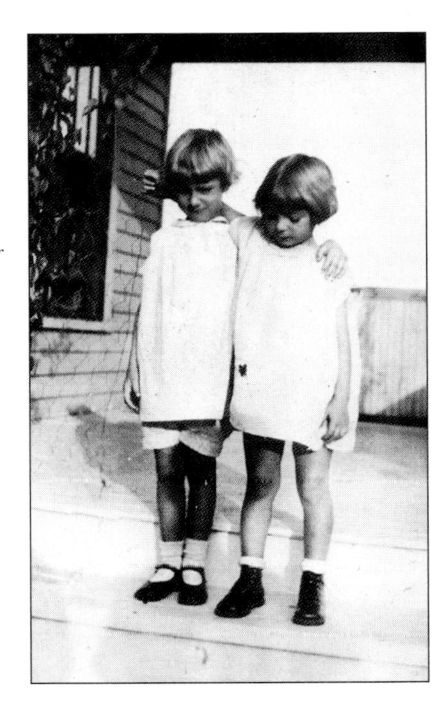

Dorothy Dauer and Julia Carnaghi Pastori are good friends ready for fun.

As we unearth each of these outlandish lessons learned from our dear mothers it is always difficult to keep from laughing. And always amid our laughter one of us invariably whispers. . .

"Yes . . . but what if?"

Angeline and Louise Carolli play with their uncle's World War I hat.

Five Garavaglia sisters reunite: Rosa, Maria, Teresina, Christina, and Palmira.

Proverbs

A serene Mary Puricelli poses in her Sunday best, circa 1920.

ccording to early Christian sources, the Bible's Book of Proverbs was also known by the name of "Wisdom." Its primary purpose was particularly directed to the young and the inexperienced. The wisdom taught covers a wide field of human and divine activity ranging from matters purely secular to the most lofty moral aspirations. The wisdom of the immigrant nonna can readily be likened to that of Solomon.

Their own special Italian proverbs also covered a wide scope of knowledge. Under the veil of their pithy sentences are hidden gems, which like tiny sparks of holy fire heap together to give life to their simple words.

These unworldly, yet profoundly learned women's words continue to teach us so much about life. Their lessons may be simple yet they are rich in substance.

Fingering their worn beads, our nonnas quietly enriched our lives with a wealth of wisdom.

Ceccha Zoia, Rosa Giudici, and Batella Puricelli meet for a coffee break.

Lucille Neri enjoys her garden in 1945.

Mary Verdi, Ann Chinicci, and Lena Torrisi return from church services.

Lena DiLiberto and Colleen Mazzola visit the Saint Louis Catherdral.

Penni non fanno uccelli. The feathers do not make the bird.

Casa senza donna, barca sensa timon. A house without a woman is a boat without a rudder.

Dio chiude una porta, ma apre un finestra. God closes one door, but opens a window.

Ride il Venerdi, piangerà la Domenica. Laugh on Friday, cry on Sunday.

Chi ha la salute é ricco, ma non lo so. He who is healthy is rich, but doesn't know it.

La bugia ha gambe corte. Lies have short legs.

Il lupo perde il pelo, mai il vizu. The wolf changes his skin, but never his vice.

Questa é la vita bella! This is the beautiful life!

La miseria guarisce la superbia. Hard times cure conceit.

Dolce é patir per chi si ama. Sacrifice is sweet for those we love.

Il vino porta gioia al cuore e felicita all' anima. Wine gladdens the heart and mellows the mind.

Chi troppo parla, spesso falla. He who talks much, errs much.

Il piatto non-si restituesci vuoto. Never return an empty plate.

Chi ama é amato. Who loves is loved.

Se fai male pensaci. Se fai bene dimentica. Do wrong and remember it. Do good and forget it.

Left to right, Adelaide Merlo, Mrs. Ceriotti, and Carolina Ceriotti celebrate with the bride, Anne Merlo.

Left to right, Annie Merlo, Lena Anthony, and Caroline Giudici dream of driving this new car, circa 1928.

Eleanor Barni looks elegant in her Easter outfit, circa 1931.

La mamma é l'anima, chi la perde non quadagna. One's mother and one's soul, when lost, can never be restored.

Chi va piano va sano é va lontano. He who goes slowly goes safely and goes far.

Il nome della mamma é bello piú del canzone d'ogni uccello. The name of mother is more beautiful than the song of any bird.

Chiu' sá meno credi. The more one learns the less gullible he is.

Helen Berra and Patricia Berra-Nappier make nonna's dolci.

U dispettu resta a lui che lo fa. Vindictiveness remains with he who is vindictive.

A ogni uccello il suo nido sembra bello. Each bird finds his nest beautiful.

Chi lascia la strada vecchia per la nuova, sa quello che lascia ma non sa quello che trova. He who leaves the old path for the new knows what he leaves but not that which he will find.

Ann Chinicci and friend show their look-alike dresses during the 1920s.

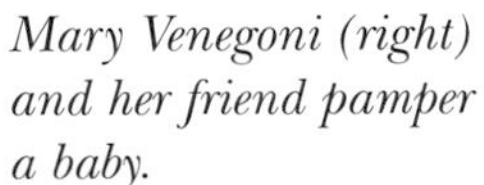

Mary Venegoni (right) and her friend pamper a baby.

Ida Carnaghi rests on her Model-T Ford, circa 1917.

Il cuore allegro é meglio di una borsa piena. A happy heart is superior to a full purse.

Baciare e abbracciare é vero Italiano. To kiss and to hug is to be a true Italian.

Baci e abbracci non fanno cicatrici. Kisses and hugs leave no scars.

La lingua non ha ossa, ma rompe il dorso d'uomo. The tongue has no bones, but it can break a man's back.

L'arvulu, guannu e nicu s' ha'drizzari, si cristci tortu poi nun c'chi fari. The tree must be straightened while it is young. If it grows up twisted then nothing more can be done.

Chi cerca trova. Who seeks, finds.

L'abito non fa il monaco. The habit does not make the monk.

Cativo amico, pessimo marito. A bad friend, a worse husband.

Mary Franceschi, 1936 St. Ambrose Church May Queen, with her handmaids.

Angelo Galli and Edith Miriani wait for the click of the camera.

Big sister Theresa Merlo and Ida Galli stand very still for their picture in 1918.

Gloria Gambaro breaks a dish to insure the bride, Clem Garavaglia, good luck.

Rose Merlo, Annie Merlo, and friends rest near a picket fence.

Theresa Spino and friends share a happy get-together.

The Sweet Side of Nonna

Saint Ambrose ladies line up, ready to serve at the Annual Ravioli Dinner in the 1970s.

Pesche Ripiene

Filled Peaches

8 peaches
6 macaroon snaps, crumbled
1/2 tsp. vanilla
2 tsp. sugar
1/2 tsp. almonds
wine – enough to make paste

Wash and halve peaches, scooping out center into a bowl. Add macaroon crumbs, sugar, wine, vanilla, and almonds then mix. Fill centers of peaches. Put open side up into a buttered baking dish. Dot with butter and bake about one hour in 350°F oven or until top is brown. Canned peaches could be used but they should be drained in a colander about one hour before using.

Crema Veneziana
Venetian Cream

1/2 cup sugar
1/2 cup flour
1/2 tsp. salt
1 2/3 cup milk
1 cup whipping cream
1 cup butter
1 tsp. vanilla
1 1/2 cups sifted powdered sugar

Combine sugar, flour, and salt in a heavy saucepan. Add milk gradually, stirring after each addition until mixture is smooth. Add cream, stirring constantly. Cook over medium heat until very thick. Boil one minute; chill until set. To speed chilling, set over ice water.

Using electric beater, cream butter and vanilla until butter is softened. Add 3/4 cup of the powdered sugar and beat until fluffy. Add chilled cream mixture alternately with remaining sugar, beating until smooth after each addition. Yields about 4 cups.

Amaretti
Macaroons

3/4 cup almonds (blanched)
2 egg whites
1/4 tsp. salt
1 cup sugar
1/2 tsp. almond extract

Chop blanched almonds. Beat egg whites and salt together. Add sugar one heaping teaspoon at a time. Beat vigorously until it forms stiff peaks. Add chopped almonds with almond extract. Drop on cookie sheet about 1 1/2 inches apart, making their size about one teaspoonful. Bake at 350°F until lightly browned.

Rulio di Ricotta

Ricotta Cheese Roll

Roll

3 eggs, separated

1 cup sugar

1 1/2 cups flour

3 tsp. baking powder

2 tbsp. melted butter

1/4 tsp. salt

1 tsp. vanilla

1/3 cup milk

Filling

1 lb. ricotta cheese

2 tsp. citron, finely minced (optional)

3/4 cup powdered sugar

1/2 cup cream, whipped

Beat egg yolks; add sugar gradually. Add butter. Add sifted dry ingredients, alternately with milk. Add vanilla. Fold in beaten egg whites. Bake on greased sheet pan, 10x16 inches. Bake at 325°F for 15 to 20 minutes. Cut off edges. Turn out onto a towel sprinkled thickly with powdered sugar and spread with filling.

Reroll and refrigerate. When ready to use, slice and sprinkle powdered sugar over top of roll.

Savoiardi

Lady Fingers

3 eggs, separated

2/3 cup powdered sugar

1/2 cup flour, sifted

1/8 tsp. salt

1/2 tsp. vanilla

Combine flour, salt, and 1/3 cup sugar. Sift; beat eggs until stiff and add rest of sugar. Fold in vanilla and egg yolks. Beat until thick and light-colored. Fold in flour and sugar mixture. Press through pastry tube on ungreased pans (paper-lined). Make strips about four inches long and a half-inch wide. Dust with powdered sugar and bake at 350°F for about 10 minutes.

Budino di Riso
Frozen Rice and Apricot Pudding

1/2 cup rice
1 quart milk
1 cup sugar
4 eggs, separated
1 tbsp. lemon juice
1 1/2 cups apricot pulp

Cook washed rice five minutes in boiling water. Drain and add to milk and 1/2 cup sugar in the top of a double boiler. Cook 50 minutes, covered. Add beaten egg yolks and cook 5 minutes longer. Cool.

Whip egg whites, lemon juice, apricot pulp, and 1/2 cup sugar until mixture holds shape. Fold into cooked rice. Freeze. Yields 8 squares, 4 inch by 1 inch.

Pan Dolce con Mandorle
Almond Cake

1 cup margarine
2 cups sugar
2 tsp. vanilla
1 tsp. almond extract
1 1/2 tsp. lemon peel, grated
4 egg yolks
3 1/4 cups cake flour
4 tsp. baking powder
1 1/2 tsp. salt
1 1/2 cups milk
4 egg whites

Cream margarine and sugar until light and fluffy. Add almond extract, lemon peel, and vanilla. Sift flour, baking powder, and salt and add to creamed mixture. Alternate with milk and beat vigorously after each mixture. Beat egg whites until stiff and fold into batter. Pour into 10-inch tube buttered pan which has been sprinkled with sliced almonds. Bake at 325°F for about 80 minutes. Allow cake to remain in pan for 10 minutes to cool.

Giuggioleni Canditi

Sesame Seed Candy

1 cup sugar
1 cup honey
1 3/4 cups sesame seeds
Peeling of 1/2 orange
1 cup finely chopped almonds

Cook sugar and honey together until it forms a soft ball when dropped in cold water (test small portion). Remove from heat. Toast sesame seeds, orange peels, and almonds in oven. Chop well and add to syrup. Stir and pour on a wet baking board. Cut into small squares when hardened.

Budino alla Romano

Roman Coffee Cream

1 tbsp. instant coffee
4 tbsp. heavy cream
3 cups ricotta cheese
4 tbsp. confectioners sugar

Combine ingredients. Beat until smooth. Chill for at least one hour. Serves 6.

Baci

Kisses

2 egg whites
1 tsp. vinegar
1/4 tsp. salt
1 tsp. vanilla
2 cups powdered sugar, sifted

Beat egg whites and add vanilla, vinegar, and salt. Beat until peaks rise. Add sugar until peaks are stiff. Drop teaspoonful 3 inches apart onto a greased cookie sheet. Bake at 300°F for 15 minutes until cream-colored.

Zabaglione

Italian Egg Nog

6 eggs
1/2 cup sugar
1 cup Marsala wine

Beat eggs and sugar until thick. Stir in wine. Pour mixture into top of double boiler and set it over simmering water. Constantly beat with rotary beater until mixture begins to thicken. Remove from heat. Serve in sherbet glasses. May be served hot or chilled.

Torta D'Amaretto
Macaroon Torte

1/2 cup shortening
2 eggs
1/2 cup coconut, flaked
1/2 box yellow cake mix
1 can of cherry pie filling

Mix all ingredients together except for pie filling. Continue to mix until they are moist enough to hold together. Pour into greased 12x18-inch pan. Bake for 20 minutes at 350°F. Cool. Pour can of cherry pie filling over baked crust. Serve with whipped cream topping.

Budino Di Ricotta
Cream Cheese Custard

1/2 lb. ricotta
1/4 cup grated milk chocolate
1/4 cup finely chopped walnuts
2 tbsp. heavy cream (more if needed)

Cream ricotta. Add chocolate and nuts; blend well. Add cream for desired consistency. Serve in sherbet glasses. Makes 4 servings.

Pan Pasquale
Easter Bread

1 pkg. dry yeast
1/4 cup lukewarm water
1/4 cup oleo or shortening
2 tbsp. sugar
4 1/2 cups flour
1 cup scalded milk
6 dyed (colored) raw eggs
2 tsp. salt
2 eggs, well-beaten

Soak yeast in lukewarm water for 5 minutes. Pour scalded milk in large bowl. Add sugar, salt, eggs, and shortening. Stir. Add softened yeast. Mix in flour. Knead well on floured board for 5 minutes.

Put dough in greased bowl. Cover and let rise for two hours or until it doubles in size. Divide dough in two strands about 20 inches long; twist together to form a ring. Pinch ends together and place ring on a greased pizza pan. Let rise for one hour until light and puffy. Brush with beaten egg.

Place uncooked colored eggs into spaces of braid. Top eggs with crisscross strips of dough. Bake at 350°F for 20 minutes. Reduce heat to 325°F and bake another 15 or 20 minutes.

GRISSINI

Bread Sticks

2/3 cup warm water
1 pkg. active dry yeast
1 tsp. salt
1 tbsp. sugar
1/4 cup soft shortening
2 cups flour, sifted
sesame seeds

Dissolve yeast in water then add salt, sugar, shortening, and half of the flour. Beat until mixture is smooth. Add the rest of the flour.

Knead on a cloth-covered board; cover with flour. Knead about 6 minutes. Cover. Allow dough to rise for one hour (until doubled) then cover completely with a towel.

Heat oven to 400°F. Divide dough in half. Cut each half in 24 pieces. Roll each piece into a pencil shape (6 to 10 inches long). Place on greased baking sheet, one inch apart. Brush with beaten egg (add 1 tablespoon water to one egg); sprinkle with sesame seeds. Bake 20 to 25 minutes. Makes 48 bread sticks.

MELE DOLCE

Baked Apples

4 apples
2 tbsp. softened butter
4 tsp. sugar
1/4 cup red wine
4 lemon slices
1 cinnamon stick

Preheat oven to 375°F. Put apples in saucepan, add wine, and cover with water. Boil apples for about 5 minutes. Remove apples and place in oven dish; pour several tablespoons of hot water into the bottom of the dish. Break up cinnamon stick; add to dish. Add lemon slices. Bake for 40 minutes; baste several times during baking.

Torta Con Uva Secca
Raisin Cake

1/2 cup shortening
1 1/2 cups sugar
2 eggs
1 cup walnuts
1 tsp. cloves
1 tsp. nutmeg
1 tsp. cinnamon
2 tsp. baking soda
2 1/2 cups flour
2 cups boiled raisins, boiled for
  15 minutes
1 1/2 cups raisin water

Mix all ingredients together. Bake at 350°F for 40 minutes.

Granita di Fragole
Strawberry Sherbet

1 cup water
1/4 cup sugar
2 cups frozen strawberries, pureed
2 tbsp. lemon juice

Bring water and sugar to boil over moderate heat; stir only until sugar dissolves. Timing from the moment the mixture begins to boil, cook for exactly 5 minutes. Remove from heat immediately and cool to room temperature. Stir in strawberries and lemon juice. Pour mixture into an ice cube tray. Freeze for 3 to 4 hours, stirring every 30 minutes. The finished granita should have a fine, snowy texture.

Cafe Napoletana
Coffee Napoli

1/2 cup coffee
1 tbsp. grated lemon rind
1 tbsp. grated orange rind
1 tsp. anise seed
3 cups water
whipped topping

Mix coffee, lemon rind, orange rind, and anise seed in the brew basket of an automatic drip coffee maker. Prepare coffee with 3 cups of water. Serve in small cups. Garnish with whipped topping.

Baci Di Donne
Kisses of Women

2 sticks butter
2 cups flour
3/4 cup sugar
8 oz. filbert nuts, ground
chocolate

Cream together butter and sugar. Mix in flour and nuts. Roll into one-inch balls. Bake in oven 325 degrees for 20 to 25 minutes. Cool and put melted chocolate between two cookies.

Croccanti
Peanut Crunchies

2 egg whites
1 tsp. baking powder
3 cups flour, sifted
3 cups sugar
3 tbsp. shortening, melted
1 lb. peanuts
2 tsp. lemon flavor extract

Mix sugar, flour, baking powder, and peanuts in large bowl. Add melted shortening and extract. Fold in egg whites (beaten stiff) Add small amount of water to moisten dough to hold together (if too soft, add a little more flour to dough). Cut about 1 1/2 inches long and 1/2 inch wide. Place on greased pans about one inch apart. Bake at 350°F for 12 to 15 minutes, until light brown. Take off pan while hot.

Pesche Nel Marsala
Marsala Peaches

1 can peach halves (1 lb. 14 oz.)
1/2 cup cream Marsala
1-inch cinnamon stick

Drain the peace halves, reserving one tablespoon syrup. In medium bowl, combine peaches, Marsala, cinnamon stick, and reserved syrup. Refrigerate covered until the peaches are very well chilled (at least 2 hours). To serve, turn peaches and liquid into individual dessert dishes. Makes 4 servings.

Biscottini
Anise Seed Cookies

4 cups flour
4 egg yolks
4 egg whites, beaten stiff
1 cup shortening
1 cup sugar
1/2 cup milk
6 tsp. baking powder
1 tbsp. vanilla
1 tbsp. anise seeds

Cream shortening and sugar. Mix egg yolks and vanilla. Add milk, dry ingredients, and seeds. Fold in egg whites. Shape into small doughnuts and bake in oven at 350°F for 15 minutes or longer. Frost with the following: 1/2 cup powdered sugar; very little water. Brush on cooled cookies.

TORTA LAMPO
Lightning Cake

2 oz. unsweetened chocolate
1/2 cup blanched almonds
1/4 cup walnuts
5 eggs, separated
3/4 cup sugar
1/2 cup strong coffee
whipped cream

Melt chocolate over hot water. Chop almonds and walnuts very fine. Beat egg yolks lightly, adding sugar, nuts, melted chocolate, and coffee. Mix well. Beat the egg whites briskly until they stand in peaks. Fold stiff egg whites gently into the chocolate mixture; fold in thoroughly.

Pour into a 9-inch cake pan that has been previously greased. Dust lightly with flour. Bake for one hour at 350°F. Cool. Serve with whipped cream or cream substitute.

TORTA D'ANGELO
Angel Pie

4 eggs
1/2 tsp. cream of tartar
1 cup whipped cream
juice of one lemon
grated rind of one lemon
1 cup sugar
salt – a few grains

Combine egg whites and cream of tartar. Beat until stiff. Add 1/2 cup of sugar; salt. Beat until stiff and glossy. Pour into well-buttered 9-inch pie tin. Bake at 225°F for 20 minutes. Increase heat to 300°F and bake for 40 minutes, then cool.

Combine egg yolks, 1/2 cup sugar, lemon juice, and rind. Cook over hot water, stirring constantly until thick and smooth. Cover shell with 1/2 cup whipped cream. Add lemon mixture then remaining whipped cream. Chill for 24 hours.

Crema Cappuccino
Coffee Pudding

1 1/2 cups coffee
1/2 cup milk
2 eggs
2 tbsp. Knox gelatin
3 tbsp. sugar
1/2 tsp. vanilla

Place coffee and gelatin in double boiler. Beat yolks and sugar then add milk. Stir into hot coffee. After it becomes like a soft custard, remove from heat and add whites of two eggs, beaten stiff. Add vanilla. Beat all together. Set to harden. Beat and reheat again. Allow to harden firmly. Serve with chopped nuts and whipped cream.

Pignolate Miele
Honey Sweets

8 eggs
1/2 cup shortening
1/2 cup sugar
5 cups flour
2 tsp. baking powder
3/4 cup honey
1 cup sugar

Beat eggs, sugar, and shortening. Add flour and baking powder which have been sifted together. Knead into a dough. Roll out like a pencil. Cut into 1/4-inch pieces. Drop a few at a time into a saucepan in hot shortening. When golden brown, remove with slotted spoon to absorbent paper. Let honey come to a boil, then add sugar and cookie bits in a large bowl. Pour hot honey over all. Stir quickly. With a tablespoon, scoop up a little at a time. Shape into balls. Build honey balls into a Christmas tree or pine cone shapes. Sprinkle with confetti sprinkles if desired.

Crostata di Ricotta

Ricotta Pie

2 lb. ricotta cheese

1 tsp. vanilla

1 cup sugar

3 eggs

2 tbsp. flour

Filling

Whip ricotta in mixer for 3 minutes. Add vanilla, sugar, and eggs. Gradually add flour.

Crust

Use 10 crushed graham crackers. Add 2 tablespoons melted butter and mix together. Press and shape in a pie dish. Add filling. Bake in a moderate (350°F) oven for 30 minutes.

Crostoli di Noci

Nut Puffs

2 egg whites

2 tsp. vinegar

1 cup sugar

1 cup dates, chopped

1 cup nuts, chopped

Beat egg whites until stiff. Mix sugar into egg whites; add vinegar and beat until stiff (7 to 8 minutes). Add dates and nuts. Drop on buttered cookie sheet. Bake in very slow oven for 30 minutes.

Biscotti di Napoli
Neapolitan Cookies

1/2 cup oil
1/2 cup sugar
3 eggs
2 cups flour
1 tsp. baking powder
1/2 cup chopped nuts
5 maraschino cherries, chopped
1/4 cup chocolate chips, chopped
1 tsp. anise flavor

Beat eggs. Beat in sugar and oil. Add sifted flour and baking powder, nuts, cherries, chips, and flavor. After ingredients are mixed, divide into four small loaves. Bake on greased cookie sheet at 350°F for 20 minutes until brown. Cut loaves on an angle sliced 1 1/2 inches wide. Bake 5 minutes more.

Torta di San Guiseppe
St. Joseph's Cake

1/2 cup heavy cream
1 cake of yeast
7 oz. flour, sifted
5 oz. butter
2 1/2 oz. sugar
grated rind of 1 lemon
4 egg yolks
4 egg whites
3 oz. raisins
3 oz. almonds
1/4 tsp. salt

Beat butter until creamy. Add flour, salt, egg yolks, sugar, and yeast. Add cream and lemon rinds, raisins, and chopped almonds. Beat until batter drops from spoon. Add stiffly beaten egg whites, mix well. Pour mixture into greased and preheated, fluted pan. Put in warm place and let rise to about double in size. Bake about one hour in moderate oven. Sprinkle with sugar while still warm.

Pan D'Anice
Anise Cake

1 pkg. yellow cake mix
5 tbsp. powdered sugar
2 tbsp. oil
2 eggs
1/3 cup sugar
1/2 tsp. anise seed, crushed
1 tsp. pure vanilla extract
1/2 tsp. anise extract

Mix all ingredients in a bowl and beat two minutes. Pour into two greased and floured 9-inch cake pans. Bake in 350°F oven for 25 to 30 minutes. Remove from pans and cool. Add 1/2 teaspoon anise extract to your favorite frosting and frost tops and side of layer cakes generously.

Granita di Mandorle
Almond Ice

3 egg whites
3/4 cup sugar
dash of salt
1/4 cup whole blanched almonds
almond extract
1 1/2 cups heavy cream
3/4 tsp. vanilla extract
12 candied cherries

Have egg whites at room temperature. Cook 1/4 cup water with sugar and salt until dissolved. Bring mixture to boiling without stirring until it spins a thread when dropped from spoon. Beat egg whites until peaks are formed. Pour the syrup mixture slowly into egg whites while beating constantly. Refrigerate covered for 30 minutes.

Place almonds in 350°F oven in shallow pan until toasted. Finely grind almonds in blender. Place in bowl and add 1 1/2 tsp. almond extract. Beat cream with 1/4 tsp. almond extract and vanilla until stiff. Fold into egg white mixture. Spoon into 12 paper-lined, 2 1/2-inch muffin pan cups. Sprinkle with almond mixture and top with cherries. Cover with foil and freeze until firm. Makes 12 servings.

Mothers

They dared to cross
Vast oceans
Far from the safety of their homes
Their beloved Italy.

They were determined
To start a new life
In a land foreign
To their hearts, their tongue
And their love

And they defied
Those who looked at them with disdain
And dared them to learn a new language. . .
To grasp a new life, raise families
Despite poverty, derision, and prejudice.

These brave women
Dared
Defied
Determined
And success was theirs

Because their shield was motherhood
Protected by an armor of faith
Facing all ills that come with life
Strengthened with the balm of gentleness
Soothing the hearts of those they love.

Daring, devoted to their cause,
Their homes, their families, and their God.

They were our mothers whose lives
Paralleled His Mother
Who also dared,
Was determined
And devoted to us
Their children of Her Son.

– Eleanore Berra Marfisi

Clementina Garavaglia poses with children Lena Moresi and Josephine Lucca, circa 1906.

Contributors

Adcock, Lisa
Aiazzi, Jo
Airoldi, Louise
Allgier, Marianne
Amoroso, Marie
Annis, Lena
Antinora, Carol
Antinora, Sr. Catherine
Barni, Josie
Belfiglio, Nick
Berra, Helen
Berra, Lance
Bertani, Jo
Bertani, Marie
Bianchi, John and Rosemary
Bommarito, Rev. Vincent
Borghi, Jim
Borghi, Rosemary
Bottini, Jane & Angelo
Calcaterra, Grace
Cattini, Dorothy
Ceriotti, Agnes
Colombo-Nettemeyer, Evelyn
Colombo, Mike and Marie
Colombo, Rose
Corso, Carlotta
Cottone, Louisa
Cuccia-Brand, Maria
Fassi, Mary
Fazio, Adriana
Floretta, Carmen
Forbes, Carol
Franceschi, Mary
Galli, Ida
Gambaro, Gloria
Garavaglia, Charles
Garavaglia, Clementine
Garavaglia, Fritz
Gartner, Beverly
Gitto, Annie
Gitto, Francesca
Gitto, Stephen
Giudici, Theresa
Grassi, Eda
Griffero, Gloria
Grimoldi, Johanna
Gualdoni, Anita
Huss, Pamela and Michael
Johnson, Jennifer
Kelso, Rose
Kemper, Donna
Kolafa, Vincent
Lahrman, Ann
Luck, Lucy
Macchi, John and Dolores
Marcallini, Judy
Mariani, Dolores
Marino, John
Marino, Joseph
Mattera, Carmelina
Mazzuca, Joseph
Mazzuca, Tony
McFall, Albina
Merlo, Patricia
Merlotti, Marie
Milani, Rose
Monolo, Debbie
Moresi-Jansen, Virginia
Neri, Lucille
Palazzolo, Annie
Parentin, Rosemary
Pastori, Julia
Petrucci, Silvana
Pisoni, Mary
Polizzi, Msgr. Sal
Pona, Virginia
Pozza, Linda
Pozzo, Mario
Pratt, Tina
Puricelli, Shirley
Ranzini, Ambrose
Ravetta, Johanna
Riganti, Laura
Rossomanno-Philips, Dorotea
Salamone, Louis
Sandhofer, Mary
Savio, Thomas
Stelzer, Carolyn
Tapella, Louise
Thompson, Mary
Tornetto, Larry
Torno, Paul
Torretta, Mary
Valli, Carole
Venegoni, James
Venezia, Ida
Viola, Louise
Zienta, Mary

Epilogue

The early immigrant Italian women were armed with pride and determination. They were as strong and unflinching as granite. Yet they retained their charming simplicity and a deep faith that defies description.

The intricate blend of their beliefs continues to fascinate the second and third generation Italian Americans. Recognizing that through the ages, their proverbs, home remedies, superstitions, and folk tales have been embellished and enhanced with a sprinkling of imagination, this treasure trove continues to be loved and jealously preserved!

Angelo and Mary Galli in a 1912 photograph.